Trumpian Abuse: Government & Family Systems that Prop-up The Male Regime

Doreen Ludwig

Copyright © 2018 Doreen Ludwig

First Edition

All rights reserved.

ISBN: Title ID: 8175172
ISBN-13: 978-1985824621

DEDICATION

To those who pursue truth.
To those who do no harm.

CONTENTS

	Acknowledgments	i
	Introduction	3
1	Historical Inequality	9
2	Due Process v. Administration	15
3	Modus Operandi	31
4	Domestic Violence v. Family Court	57
5	Community Fatherhood v. Family Court Outcomes	77
6	Contested Custody v. Dispute Resolution	93
7	Special Interests v. Truth & Justice	115
8	Conclusion	135

ACKNOWLEDGMENTS

I thank those who believed this work could make a difference.
I thank David Miller, for listening, for accepting, for believing, for showing me genuine love..
I thank all the advocate moms for their help and input.

INTRODUCTION

When I published my first book *"Motherless America: Confronting Welfare's Fatherhood Custody Program"* I believed telling my experience - presenting research that showed our federal government funds preference for custody awards to unfit fathers - would begin a movement of education and reform. I was naive. I did not fathom the scope of self-interests that would actively mute and bury my work. Ironically - even though I left an abusive father – domestic violence affiliates became the largest special interest working to undermine and silence knowledge.

This second book is my resolve to be heard above the dim of powerful people invested in the status quo. I realize that my work may get suppressed by those with ulterior motives.

I am providing the research for free. Later, I may re-issue this book and add to the work. For now, I beg women and those that care about integrity in government systems – READ!

Trumpian Abuse: Government & Family Systems that Prop-up the Male Regime presents documents that formed *Motherless America*. By layering reports and articles, I show a government system – family court – that props-up the male regime – patriarchy in the home. I show how domestic violence interests assist.

I hope that one day someone will make change from what is contained herein.

The Challenge

This book is about women who have underage children and no longer want relationships with the children's dad.

This book is about women and children who have suffered abuse from the male that they loved. Adult women who believed "Stop the relationship - stop the hitting, demeaning words, control tactics and incest."

This book presents a system designed to put power in the hands of the oppressor – to keep children property of males - to punish women who feel that an abusive dad is best kept at bay.

This book asks questions. It asks you to think - to challenge your perceptions about how families and systems interact and function.

> **Whose** role is important? What happens when one person views themselves superior?
>
> **How** does society view children? Are they property of adults or beings unto themselves?
>
> **What** is important to a child's mental and physical health?
>
> **How** do childhood circumstances impact adult attitudes and behaviors?
>
> **When** a child and parent's interests are in contradiction, who is prioritized?

This book asks you to think about government systems - how policies impact day-to-day lives and events.

This book requires you to delve into abuse – what it is and why it is perpetrated. This will be difficult as abuse is often abhorrent. We will explore abuse's darkest depths and look at its existence in the most sanctimonious of relationships: family and government.

Read this book.
Challenge yourself.
Put aside preconceived perceptions.
Broaden your knowledge and ideas.
Consider solutions.
Determine: Change abuse - Better the world.

Question Equality

What is women's equality? Is it autonomy - the right to make her own decisions?

Is a woman who stays in her traditional gender role less valuable than a man?

Is cooking, cleaning, having and raising children, less important than a job that generates a paycheck?

Is woman's equality only for women working outside the home?

Does giving birth make a woman beholden to the male?

If she bears a child must she permit the male to control? Is she required to give up her autonomy? Become subservient?

Should equality and autonomy extend to the home front?

Is "women's work" insignificant and easily replaced?

Is devaluing motherhood abusive and oppressive?

Question The Problem

Would you believe that tens of thousands of mothers each year are being told their role of primary caregiver has no meaning and should not continue if they leave abuse?

Women who decided to leave a man who devalued them.

Women who discovered incest.

Women who left alcoholics and drug abusers.

Women who felt verbal and physical assaults - demeaning treatment and words - sneaky manipulations meant to control - were, ultimately, unhealthy for their child.

Women who have been primary caretakers, stay-at-home moms, assuming almost 100% of child care and housekeeping duties are suddenly being court-ordered to "share parenting" or "co-parent."

- Because she persists in trying to keep him and his harm from their kids.
- Because she is truly afraid.
- Because she believes she makes better educational, medical and experience decisions.
- Because she thinks she should continue as the primary caregiver even after leaving.
- Because abusive men never stop and often escalate their insidious harm.

Mothers are losing all contact with children they nurtured until entering family court. At best - mothers are relegated to secondary stand-ins - ordered to shut-up when harm stems from daddy.

Do we assume that these men have never been asked to help?

Why do we assume that a male who has never parented is fit?

That he will excel at healthy meal preparation, arrange doctor visits, wash laundry, change bedsheets, carry out a calm, nurturing bedtime routine?

How quick will he become an accomplished parent?

Can an 800 telephone line, a book, or a 2-8 week course, prepare an uninvolved dad for the day-to-day chores involved in raising well-balanced, stable kids?

Do children thrive when routines and caregiving are radically changed nightly or weekly?

Is co-parenting fair to a well-adjusted child? What about a child raised in a home full of turmoil?

Why Trumpian Abuse?

The title of this book is not a political renouncement. Trumpian Abuse is a behavioral analogy – a still-to-unfold historical viewpoint. President Trump is an outcome of our dominant society. America permits people to use nefarious means to stay on-top and in control – to pursue and retain wealth and power. Anger, disenfranchisement, resentment and fear is felt by those at the receiving end of purposeful inequality – harm and maltreatment – so they align themselves with the strong man, the manipulator, the obtuse. The privileged wear blinders and scream for more self-advantage rather than be a voice for the oppressed. Disparity escalates. Rage compounds. Abuse persists and envelops even more as American institutions continue to operate for the benefit of the corrupt, the few, instead of the common good. This book highlights one venue – family court – where abuse is an advantage.

Trump: "to defeat or outdo a competitor by bringing a valuable resource or advantage into play."

Characteristics of Trumpian Abuse belong to –

the all-out self-important, no holds barred attack,
the "I'm never wrong,"
the "hit back ten times harder"
the racist,
the misogynist,
the litigator,
the psychological manipulator,
the rich,
the powerful,
the well-connected,
the one who must prevail regardless of cost to self and others.

CHAPTER ONE

Historical Inequality

The tradition of "coverture" meant women who married became legal property of their husbands. Women lost individuality and personal property rights to their husband. He was permitted to beat and otherwise punish her. If she bore children, they became his property too. A married woman was not permitted to take her children away from her husband, without his assent, even if he was incestuous.

It wasn't until 1966 that the U.S. Supreme Court ruled coverture obsolete. Margot Canaday, who writes about gender rights and the law, states *"Coverture's demise blunted (even if it did not eliminate) male privilege within marriage."*[1]

The shift from viewing women as property of males is a recent occurrence fostered by the Civil Rights Amendment and the rise of the women's movement. Domestic Violence movements developed alongside since physical violence is one of the most visible abuses of male privilege. However, **domestic violence and women's freedom or autonomy movements are not one and the same**. Freedom to live without physical abuse is not the same as the freedom to control your life, to own property, to nurture and protect children, and to leave a relationship if it is not in your and your child's best interests.

Women's Rights v. Men's Rights

A right implies ownership. The women's rights movement

---

[1] Canaday, Margot (2008). "Heterosexuality as a legal regime". In Michael Grossberg & Christopher L. Tomlins. The Twentieth Century and After (1920—). The Cambridge History of Law in America. 3. Cambridge, UK: Cambridge University Press, page 445

coalesced around the simple notion that women were not to be owned by males. Women wanted self-ownership. Men were not free to subordinate wives. If a woman chose to work she was permitted to do so and to keep her paycheck (under coverture he owned any money she earned). Women entered the workforce. They wanted jobs held by men. They wanted to make decisions and influence outcomes. They wanted equal rights – freedom from oppression.

Let's be honest. Not all men treated their wives and children poorly. But many men - the disenfranchised and the powerful - felt threatened by these vocal ladies. Many men clung to notions of women's usefulness being limited to servant or sex partner. Those men rationalized their hatred - calling newly empowered females "Feminazi's" - working to imply "feminist" was a negative term, that feminists undermined the societal order, did not know their place, were men haters. Men were empowered by women such as Phyllis Schlafly, successful Christian conservative opponent of the Equal Rights Amendment, who felt giving women equality by constitutional amendment would undermine the family. Schlafly promoted "family values" and the idea that women belonged in the home. She undermined the fight for equality by igniting the differences between wives, mothers, and professionally employed females by claiming feminists "did not speak for them." Schlafly became an integral asset of the father's rights movement.

Backlash flourished even while women made huge strides towards equality. Men worked hard to retain dominance. Domestic Violence groups set-up temporary shelters for the physically attacked. They fought for greater criminal prosecution of relationship assault victims. They embraced legal "protection" orders in lieu of jail terms. However, they left children out of the equation - failed to see the corollaries between treatment of mothers and their children, the wider matrix of abuse, the motivation for protection that children provide, and the principle of ownership as an impetus of mistreatment.

The women's rights movement focused their attention on outside-the-home advancements – achieving employment parity and protection. Advocacy and advancement became the venue of single women, those who choose not to have children. In the 1970's women with young children rarely pursued careers, they waited until the children grew up. As time progressed and economics demanded, working motherhood became commonplace. This led to wider calls for men to help out with household duties – meals, dishes, cleaning, even child care – and demand for quality paid child care. These two home life advancements – paid child care and husband participation – are now commonly accepted by young women who, until the Trump presidency, did not even consider women's inequality to be a political concern.

Even women's rights groups seem to have taken women's equality in the home for granted – or they have left these mothers out in the cold, preferring to pursue gender equality based on sexual orientation rather than roles and treatment within a traditional family unit. Women's rights and domestic violence movements relinquished women with children to "family values."

Father Supremacy - Organizing and Funding

Silence regarding primary caregiving mothers and children from these two groups enabled the growth of a specifically tailored men's rights concern called "Father's Rights." Divorce became a frequent choice for women expressing newfound autonomy. Women with young children did not hesitate when they found home life unconscionable. Ironically, children stirred action as mom realized there could be negative consequences if she stayed. At first, the legal system favored most of these mothers. Divorce laws forced disclosure of home events that prompted dissolution – violence and mistreatment by males was a serious consideration when awarding custody of children. Stability and continuity of primary care, still the forte of mothers, was commonplace in custody determinations, with men being given part-tme visitation.

Men were losing ownership of not only women, but children. Fathers were losing their "rights." Father's rights groups (FRs) organized to combat this loss of privilege. FRs lobbied for changes in support and custody laws, created research to substantiate their superiority in the family, built networks of family court professionals committed to father's rights, and disseminated legal tactics guaranteed to "win."

Patriarchal groups such as the National Fatherhood Institute (NFI) spent millions per year on education and lobbying in an effort to impede women's progress.

Patriarchs infiltrated private endowments earmarking funds for the promotion of father's rights goals.

Politicians advanced the agenda by allocating fatherhood monies, secretly funding custody litigation outcomes to favor men, all the while omitting protection from trumpian abuse for mothers and children.

Like any group on the losing side of an equality movement, dads portrayed an image of victimization and discrimination against men via family court and in domestic violence situations.

Conclusion

This book looks at one system – Family Court. Admittedly, decent dads are harmed by this for-profit system. In an economic formula abuse generates the profit. However, this book emanates from an abused female perspective. Truly abused dads comprise a low percentage of cases. Trumpian abusers are adept at litigation tactics that turn victims into perpetrators.

My desire is to open the system to critique – to accountability – not to veer it to favor one gender - but to shed light on corruption, fueled by those who practice trumpian abuse.

This book details the systems within the system. It explains how they operate, who built the system currently presented, who funds it, and the interplay of internal operators.

This book points out errors in the current structure – including how we think about relationship harm.

CHAPTER TWO

Due Process v. Administration

When parents dissolve a relationship they must determine who will care for any minor children. Where will the child live? Who will be responsible for education, health care, and the mundane tasks of life? How much control and involvement comes from the second parent?

The majority of dissolving parents reach an agreement without the aid of outsiders. Those parents usually stay with the model of care that existed prior to split. Since mothers handle the vast majority of care, mothers frequently retain primary custody - the children reside at her home during the week and visit dad every other weekend. The children may spend a few hours with father during the week. Dad is free to attend activities like sports and shows. Dad is free to speak by telephone. Parents who both have well-paying, demanding jobs often opt for shared parenting agreements where the child is moved between homes in equal amounts of time. Parents adjust and maintain an atmosphere of peace in order to give children the stability they need to grow into adulthood. Parents make difficult circumstances work. Parents do not "sweat the small stuff." Parents do not micro-manage each other's life.

Who contests custody?

For those with severe abusive personality traits, giving the other parent autonomy and basic respect is impossible. Abusers objectify others – they exist for them – not as separate individuals. Abusers love asserting authority. Abusers demean. They mock. They hurt. They control. They obsess. They demand.

They harass. They threaten. They escalate. They litigate.

An abuser will never resolve a question of custody unless they win. It doesn't matter if he never participated in parenting. He wants an agreement that benefits him. He fights for shared parenting because he will not have to pay support. He demands primary custody to gain power. He wants his children to conform to his whims. He wants to show he is in charge – mother is nothing compared to the power he wields.

When you have two parents required to form a custody agreement, the greater the level of abuse - the lower the chance of their reaching a satisfactory arrangement. Because one parent intends to use the agreement for reprehensible purposes, this pair will rarely reach a satisfactory plan.

Abused women do one of two things – they concede or they fight. She may agree to give him half parenting because the court has shown a clear preference for that option. She may live with his antics. However, if she feels that harm to her child outweighs her own hesitance, she will fight for primary custody. She will initially believe speaking up will insulate - authorities will act in favor of protecting the innocent. She will most certainly believe any evidence she holds will be heard. She puts her faith in family court and lets her case unfold.

How does family court operate?

An abused mother does not comprehend that accepted rules of evidence and law do not apply in family court. She believes, and may have been assured by a lawyer, that her case will play out along the lines of a criminal case – evidence is presented, the opposing party can refute the charges, but in the end, the truth will prevail.

The Family Court Conundrum

However, family court is a conundrum. Because it operates under the Department of Health and Human Services, (HHS) rather than the Department of Justice (DOJ) is more a social service than an arm of justice. Complicating the matter, many states operate family court as part of their judicial system, yet run parallel social service operations in conjunction with court functions. Child Welfare (also called Child Protection, Child Services, Children and Youth) uses family court orders to enforce taking away children through foster care or adoptions. Child Support Enforcement operates alongside family court – acting as an intermediary for custody decisions. While the bulk of judicial functions are left to administration units, decisions are legally sanctioned and enforceable via signed judicial orders.

Because they have assumed the majority of child care duties, typically, mothers are the "custodial" parent at the onset of litigation. Fathers must legally request a different make-up. Fathers may ask to be primary physical custodian – the child will spend the bulk of time living with dad. Fathers may request joint physical custody – the child will live with each parent in equal allotments. Fathers may request primary legal custody - authority to determine the path of major life choices and needs. Parents who cannot mutually agree to a custody schedule will be left to the mercy of the court and its administrative process. Failure to abide by the judicial order subjects parents to contempt, comparable to a criminal conviction.

When parents cannot agree to a custody arrangement, family court assigns a judge. Parents do not receive a jury trial. One person alone decides the family's future. Administrative units assist. Courts farm out building of the record – evidence judges use to issue an order. A judge is supposed to look at evidence and ask which person makes the better parent. A judge is supposed to write an opinion and explain his conclusion – back it up with fact and law. Because these are complex, time-involved duties, family court judges yielded responsibility to fee-driven affiliates. Mental health professionals lobbied to be appointed evaluators. The

American Psychological Association (APA) created guidelines for custody evaluations requiring the verification of facts (evidence) by way of collateral witnesses; assessment of parenting ability; and, the parent/child "fit." Strict adherence to APA guidelines is deemed ethical. Stepping outside of the industry standard is considered unethical. The industry was built around the premise that a mental health professional could quantify who deserved custody.

A hidden world of for-profit pariahs latched onto family court's increased reliance on administrative means. Lawyers found they could hide and manufacture evidence by substituting due process with office decision-making. No one would oversee or record the events and answers that contributed to custody determinations. Hefty fees paid for evaluations created an incentive. Friendships and affiliations built a network of insiders who work together to get outcomes favorable to specific clients. Local court power elite could operate without monitor. Special interest groups thrived in this unregulated environment.

Father's Rights Influence

As divorced dads became obligated to pay support they networked and formed father's rights groups to advance their interests. Founders of the father's rights movement were born in a time of patriarchy, the 1950's. They work to hold onto male privilege. A major goal of the father's rights movement is preservation of male income after divorce. They work to mitigate the financial damages of settlement and support obligation. Many early father's rights organizers blame their mothers for the loss of their own fathers. They discount women's reasons for leaving. They despise feminists and women's equality.

Founders consist of lawyers, professors and psychologists. President of the American Coalition of Fathers and Children (ACFC), Stephen Baskerville, is an associate professor of political science. Baskerville claims courts are one-sided and that mothers who initiate divorce when there are children make a "power-grab" in order to gain custody and child support payments.

Jeffrey Leving, a Chicago-area attorney, pioneered the father's rights movement claiming to stand for equality and due process for dads. Leving hosts several local radio shows and has written three books - most notably *"Divorce Wars: A Field Guide to Winning Tactics, Preemptive Strikes, and Top Maneuvers When Divorce Gets Ugly."* Leving markets father's rights ideology and organizes lobbying efforts through his website http://www.dadsrights.com/ Leving worked with President Obama in Chicago and is a participant on federal fatherhood program task forces.

A psychologist, Dr. Richard Warshak, advocates for father's rights by promoting "mediation" as a means of settling contested custody. Warshak is the author of a premier father's rights custody manual, *"Divorce Poison: How to Protect Your Family From Bad Mouthing and Brainwashing."* Warshak is a presenter at AFCC trade association conferences. He has been a board member of ACFC. He promotes the theory of Parental Alienation – a legal tactic used to silence mothers and children who protest father's physical, psychological and sexual assaults.

These three father's rights founders and many others have been instrumental in building a network of family court insiders who favor father's and dismiss complaints and evidence of maltreatment.[2]

According to Dr. Leora Rosen, author of *"The Hostage Child: Sex*

---

[2] https://en.wikipedia.org/wiki/Fathers%27_rights_movement
https://en.wikipedia.org/wiki/Stephen_Baskerville
https://en.wikipedia.org/wiki/Jeffery_M._Leving
 https://www.amazon.com/Divorce-Wars-Winning-Preemptive-Maneuvers/dp/0061121762
http://www.warshak.com/
https://www.amazon.com/Divorce-Poison-New-Updated-Bad-mouthing/dp/0061863262

Abuse Allegations in Custody Disputes" and *"Beyond The Hostage Child: Towards Empowering Protective Parents,"* father's rights is backlash. Men who felt threatened by real or perceived loss of power, resources and authority sought peer groups to shore up their opposition to women's empowerment. Their fear increases when they get divorced. That's when they feel threatened; especially abusers who are heavily invested in control. Father's rights groups can be compared to white supremacist groups because both are concerned with keeping white male identity and privilege. These two groups have similar constituencies - men who feel vulnerable, victimized and uncertain about masculinity in contemporary society. They feel entitled to power and authority over minority racial groups and genders - those they feel are beneath them.[3]

In addition to numerous books, father's rights groups market their political lobbying and legal maneuvering by way of the internet. Dr. Rosen and colleagues analyzed hundreds of men's rights and father's rights websites, categorizing themes and recording repetition of specific topics. Father's rights promote automatic shared parenting or joint custody awards. They claim they are for "children's rights" and that shared parenting awards give children the right to a father. They minimize domestic violence and men's culpability. Father's rights assert that women make false allegations of abuse in order to gain an upper hand in custody. Father's rights complain that support amounts are excessive and a way for states to make money. Father's rights promote parental alienation and other euphemisms meant to psychologically label mother as unfit for custody or purposely attempting to obliterate father's contact with his children.

---

[3] http://www.iupress.indiana.edu/product_info.php?products_id=19678
https://www.amazon.com/Beyond-Hostage-Child-Empowering-Protective/dp/1500551996
"Father's Rights Groups: Demographic Correlates and Impact on Custody Policy," Rosen, Dragiewicz, Gibbs, 2009

Father's rights claim women are equally or more violent than men - a viewpoint has been refuted by The Southern Poverty Law Center.

> "Misogynists in the men's and fathers' rights movements have developed a set of claims about women to support their depictions of them as violent liars and manipulators of men. Some suggest that women attack men, even sexually, just as much as men attack women. Others claim that vast numbers of reported rapes of women, as much as half or even more, are fabrications designed to destroy men they don't like or to gain the upper hand in contested custody cases. What follows is a brief look at some of these claims and what the best science really shows."[4]

An article entitled "Guide: How Fathers Can Win Child Custody" was retrieved by this author in 2009 from the website "Intellectual Conservative Politics and Philosophy."[5] The article refers readers to Arizona Father's Rights and related attorneys and coaches.

> *"laws are set up to award custody to the parent who has had the most involvement so far raising the child, which means the parent who has worked less - this is virtually always the mother...Since child support is mandatory, you will be paying several hundred dollars in child support to her each month. Now does that make sense? It only makes sense in the past, when you were still together as a couple... mother most likely had a less demanding job and spent more time with the children... courts usually require single mothers to obtain a full-time job that will most likely pay less than yours, why should she still be seen as more fit to take care of the*

---

[4] Article posted at https://www.splcenter.org/fighting-hate/intelligence-report/2012/men%E2%80%99s-rights-movement-spreads-false-claims-about-women
[5] File of Doreen Ludwig

children?"

The post advises dads to fight for primary custody because *"it is just as easy for you to find relatives and babysitters."* Besides telling men to fight for custody in order to avoid paying support, the article stresses the advantage of child tax credits. Tactics to win custody include: hire an aggressive lawyer; persevere – money and emotional stress will wear your ex down; and, build a case using the testimony of experts.

> *"Find a psychologist who has a reputation for being favorable to fathers and preferably one on the court's approved list. You may want to give the psychologist leading questions to ask your child, such as whether your child would prefer living with you if mother abuses drugs alcohol or smoking in front of the child, whatever bad things your child has indicated to you about living with your ex. If the results are favorable, and you have begun building up a case against your ex, that is when you want to file for a change of custody."*

This type of marketing of legal and mental health services causes many dads to pay litigators in anticipation of financial gain. Meanwhile, those same men find themselves indebted to lawyers and court appointees, sometimes on the losing end of custody awards. Those men become even more enraged. They continue to rile against a system they assert favors mothers.

While father's rights group members come and go – their cases end - practitioners stay and find new clients. Lawyers advertise they represent "father's rights." Professors use their forum to publish to advance their cause. Psychologists market labels, therapies and tests to deem mom incompetent. Father's rights ideologues have found a welcoming home in family court.

Making the Fringe the Standard

Family court provides a fertile field for abuse. Family court is steadfastly hierarchical. A judge holds absolute power. Litigants are subordinate. A tradition of patriarchy remains in the legal environment. Women are still considered beneath their male counterparts. Women's work of home and child care is devalued, yet praised when a male professes to want to perform it. Dads who litigate are automatically held in a favorable light. Dads are desired. Dads are rewarded for wanting to be a father even when abuse exists. Dad's statements are accepted as truth. Resistance from mom is seen as vindictive and disruptive.

Missing from father's rights propaganda is any mention of child care – the need for high quality education and health care; healthy food, suitable housing and safe neighborhoods.

The Fatherhood Field: Making Father's Count[6]

How can you guarantee judicial custody outcomes will favor dads?
- Go in the back door – the child support office.
- Build a public relations campaign and stockpile skewed research to convince policymakers and the public that all children need a father because fatherless kids will be criminals, drug-addicts, mentally deranged, unproductive and unhappy.
- Build a network of court appointees that believe mother's protection and resistance is more harmful than father's wrongdoing.
- Change the administration of child support to include custody outcomes favoring males. Construct fatherhood programs that partner with family court.
- Pay for it all with public and private money.

---

[6] Making Fathers Count: Assessing the Progress of Responsible Fatherhood Efforts" Annie E. Casey Foundation, Sylvester, Reich, 2002
http://www.aecf.org/KnowledgeCenter/Publications.aspx?pubguid={5931A803-4E1C-421B-844C-65644D6968E6}

The fatherhood movement shifted the dialogue. Unlike fathers' rights groups whose hatred and violence was worn on their sleeves, the fatherhood field "cleaned up" the attack by shifting the focus. Father's rights wanted to control and continue ownership of women and children. In a highly successful sleight of hand, the fatherhood movement delivered by masking those goals with concern for low-income men.

A world of propaganda against single mothers is created by the fatherhood industry. Fathers are exalted. Mothers are demonized. Mothers and children need men. Men who hit. Alcoholics. Promiscuous men. Drug addicts. Molesters. Thieves. Murderers. No behavior is too extreme. No single mother is safe. A curious and distinct lack of concern for those affected by woeful acts exists within the fatherhood industry. The fatherhood movement is an outgrowth of father's rights and conservative patriarchy, another effort at keeping mothers and children subservient, beholden to male whims and control. Their welfare is wholly dependent on him.

A comprehensive history of the fatherhood movement, *Making Fathers Count*, outlines the immense funding stream of private and public money dedicated to elevating men by way of child custody.

In the 1980s father absence became a public concern,

> *" ...as more women entered the workforce the rise of two-worker families intensified public concern about children growing up without enough attention from their parents. The dramatic increase in divorce separated even more fathers from their children gave rise to the "father's rights" movement formed by men alleging unfair treatment in court in child custody and divorce agreements."* (pages 4,5)
>
> *"At the same time the issue of family breakdown was*

becoming a topic of national conversation. The emergence of the Christian right – with their emphasis on traditional families, moral values, and committed parenting – was a clear reaction to what many people saw as a crisis of the American family. Indeed, among the first to speak out about the issue were conservatives." (page 5)

Two bastions exist within the fatherhood movement. Each works to put men in a strong position within the family. The two ideologies feed off each other – one's goal supports the others. The more nefarious group, the National Fatherhood Initiative, stems from an extreme right political stance. It operates under the radar, hiding behind minority males, all the while reshaping federal policy to favor controlling men.

1. <u>National Partnership for Community Leadership (NPCL)</u> – Comprised of community and church organizations that help low-income, minority men who have children. Many are young and unmarried. Many have criminal records. They may have records of domestic violence. They tend to have low levels of education and job skills. They are usually obligated to pay support as many mothers apply for public assistance. Changing the support office to include awards of custody and lower support helps these men.

2. <u>National Fatherhood Initiative (NFI)</u> — Comprised of high income and education white male ideologues – evangelicals, conservatives, patriarchs, male supremacists, father's rights. Since 1994, using over $2million/year, NFI operates a public education campaign to convince the public that males are essential to women and children. NFI hides an agenda of subjugation of women and children, punishment for those who leave abusive men, and custody awards for dads instead of support obligation.

Wade Horn is a founding member of NFI. Horn used his position as Assistant Secretary of Children and Families under President George W. Bush to rewrite Child Support and Child Protective Services rules to favor marriage and father custody awards. While a federal employee, Horn gave NFI over $5 million in HHS grants and contracts. Horn left the Bush administration in 2007 and joined Deloitte Consulting's Health and Human Services department, receiving HHS contracts and advising states how to set-up social service programs. Horn currently works with the Trump administration. In July, 2017, HHS granted Deloitte a 2-month, $1 million contract to "reimagine" HHS. Deloitte employees have been running "innovation" workshops since May. [7]

The fatherhood movement contains a hidden objective: to retain male domination over women and children regardless of her reasons for dismissing him. Marriage promotion is partnered with fatherhood – marriage is seen as the ultimate goal because marriage is the best way to ensure a father stays involved in his child's life (page 49). Women who refuse to stay married are punished by loss of their children.

Creating Favorable Fatherhood Research

The National Center on Fathers and Families (NCOFF) is a policy research center at the University of Pennsylvania. NCOFF was at the forefront of fostering beneficial fatherhood research through relationships with federal research bodies such as the National Institute of Child Health and Human Development, and through affiliations with academics at universities around the nation. It was a long-standing practice of father's rights groups to fund, disseminate, and advance the accumulation of bent research.

[7] http://www.motherjones.com/politics/2017/08/controversial-culture-warrior-lands-mystery-job-in-the-trump-administration/

NCOFF President Ralph Smith left NCOFF for Annie E. Casey Foundation to become the premier private foundation funder of fatherhood promotion. Smith directed Casey's large endowment away from funding need and impact child welfare programs such as after-school programs and summer camps, towards promoting fatherhood through grants to NFI's ad council media campaign, to NCOFF for fatherhood research, and to back legislation meant to accelerate father's rights and fatherhood goals.

NCOFF's research omits domestic violence, alcoholism, drug addiction, promiscuity, chronic unemployment, sexual abuse, psychological cruelty - behaviors that would contribute to adverse outcomes. Recently NCOFF's Fatherlit database has been cleaned up – old research taken off-line. *"Conceptualizing and Measuring Father Involvement"*[8] offers a compendium of fatherhood research and its venues, for those interested in comprehensive examination of the ideology that built fatherhood policy.

Why would an ivy league school be a center for biased research? Is the generation of research that claims favorable outcomes when dad retains involvement, yet which omits factors that contribute to unfavorable outcomes, unethical? How many other institutions of learning mimic this tendency?

Fatherhood and Abuse

Fatherhood proponents admit they do not know how to address domestic violence. Ironically, severe maltreatment and common misbehaviors have been ignored by the fatherhood movement

---

[8] Conceptualizing and Measuring Father Involvement, Randal Day, Michael Lamb;https://books.google.com/books?id=yQyQAgAAQBAJ&pg=PT443&lpg=PT443&dq=ncoff&source=bl&ots=xALQ_TF6N_&sig=4OgnPBHzw2SgspxOn811kUG4RHs&hl=en&sa=X&ved=0ahUKEwj78Yf7lK7ZAhWIqIMKHcRQDZIQ6AEIVTAJ#v=onepage&q=ncoff&f=false

(pages 50, 51). Oliver Williams of the Minnesota University School of Social Work's Center on Domestic Violence and the African American Community says the subject (of abuse) is one "most of the fatherhood field resists addressing" "they would rather talk about mutual violence than male responsibility." NCOFF's President admits the fatherhood field lacks standards, best practices, and review.

Billed as concern for low-income, absent dads, the fatherhood message centered on seven areas:
- fathers care about their kids;
- father's matter to children;
- joblessness and unemployment impede father's ability to pay child support;
- systemic barriers in the child support policy impede father's contact with, and interest in, their child;
- co-parenting is optimum;
- fathers need support to transition to the role of dad;
- fathers can learn and perform parenting duties through intergenerational learning (grandparents).

These seven "core learnings" outline the steps used to orchestrate a change in family court cultures that holds criminal dads in a higher light than a full-time mother; that awards custody to any father willing to litigate. Although the movement professes concern for jobless men, a review of several program reports confirms custody assistance is the primary service.

Making Father's Count, pages 58–71, contains a chronology of the people, institutions and funding that contributed to building this massive patriarchy industry.

Like the father's rights movement, the cleaned-up fatherhood movement lacks concern for children's needs of high quality education, safe communities, health care, housing and healthy food. Willis Bright of the Lilly Endowment says "I would like to see the different elements of the men's rights movement ...come together and take on an advocacy agenda on behalf of children's – whether health or education – ....that would be a powerful thing." (page 54)

The lack of appreciation of factors necessary for children to enjoy a safe, stable and nurturing youth is a major indicator of whether or not a dad truly desires to be a good parent or whether that dad is motivated by control and financial profit. Father's rights members complain [extracted from facebook comments] "I can't talk to my son but I pay for her unemployment" and "I pay support and she has a housekeeper and gardener." In contrast, mothers protest about the child abuse endured because dad is given control. Dad's rile against "the b**ch" and "the "c**t." Moms reiterate the harm being done to their child that they are incapable of stopping.

On pages 76-82 we find a list of national fatherhood groups. Children's Rights Council (CRC) is a key father's rights umbrella group.

Men have an immense complex advancing the patriarchy.

CHAPTER THREE

Modus Operandi

Fatherhood is the excuse. Access for disenfranchised dads is really access for profiteers. Concern for low-income dads struggling to pay support is a cover for men determined to hold-on to copious current and future financial assets. Federal and private fatherhood money is the conduit for industry insiders to infiltrate family court through administrative procedure.

The racket is uncovered by analyzing protocols and fatherhood publications. There are five (5) primary documents that highlight the scheme. Every sentence in every report proves the nefarious nature of a program designed to subvert custody statutes. Below is a brief overview.

OFFICE OF CHILD SUPPORT ENFORCEMENT (OCSE) GUIDELINES

Three documents that show us the framework for family court operations were generated as part of the fatherhood access/visitation (AV) program. The first two were produced in the beginning years of federal funding. *Promising Practices* was compiled in 2001 & 2002, and *Strategic Planning Guide* was published in 2006. Jessica Pearson, an AFCC affiliate and frequent presenter at father's rights conferences, was contracted to author these two playbooks. To this day, Pearson maintains a lucrative position writing OCSE protocols.

1 - Promising Practices – Common Practices[9]

Promising Practices is the foundation on which family court fatherhood programs have been built. Pearson, working under OCSE contract, amassed a variety of ways local jurisdictions increased custody for dads. Many programs existed before PRWORA having been funded by private fatherhood sources and trial federal grants. Those "promising practices" were then marketed thru a variety of vehicles to other court jurisdictions. The methods elicited have become standard - "common practices." Because *Promising Practices* is an early fatherhood production, it contains significant references which show fathers are intended to be the sole beneficiaries. Pearson admits the programs have no built-in accountability; data collection and outcome measure. Pearson blames the lack of scientific standard on a dearth of funding (page *vi*).

While federal OCSE staff, Michael Hayes (previously employed by the Texas Fragile Families Initiative, pages 45,46, *Making Fathers Count,* and as Manager of Collaborations, Fatherhood and Family Initiatives, Child Support Division, Office of Texas Attorney General), states OCSE merely offers program "guidance" and the report contains a policy disclaimer - OCSE Project Officer Debra Pontisso assisted in the production of this pre-eminent program construction document. Pontisso is significant because she is the author of AV Jurisdictional Profile guidelines which negate laws that require sexual abuse of children and other harmful acts to be a reason for losing custody. Pontisso, along with Pearson and Anita Stuckey (Texas AV grant coordinator), co-presented a workshop called "Integrating Custody Into Child Support" at the 2007 AFCC conference entitled "Children of Separation and Divorce: The Politics of Policy, Practice and Parenting."

The father's rights and fatherhood field footprint is found on page

---

[9] Promising Practices: "Access/Visitation Programs: Promising Practices," Pearson, 2001/2002. Referred to as "Promising Practices"

3, *"Promoting Greater Parent Involvement, Supplementing the federal AV activities include...supportive services for advocacy groups which have lobbied for joint custody legislation, federal acknowledgement of custody and visitation issues, and direct services for fathers seeking to strengthen ties to their children."*

Promising Practices builds on the fatherhood field's goal of increasing custody by way of the support office. *Promising Practices* focuses on six program areas: support office; prison population; high conflict families; enforcement of custody orders; faith-based groups; and, rural populations.

Section I, Introduction and Background (pages 1-9), reiterates ideology, on-going programs, and funding sources, much of which is documented within the pages of *Making Father's Count*.

Section 2, Services for IV-D Population (pages 11-24), explains how support offices were re-designed to use court appointees, acting under the guise of mediation and education, to increase father's custody. Automatic custody increases for non-custodial parents (mostly men) became the new standard with services provided by court affiliates rather than judicial adjudication. Page 18 is of interest because under *"Inducing Custodial Parents to Participate,"* Pearson recognizes the problem of primary parents not wanting to give custody to a non-caregiving parent. The answer is to *"assist the father with filing a pro se motion for visitation. This type of filing triggers a court appearance by both parents, at which time the judge will order the parties to mediation."* This statement highlights a now common practice. Judges order parents who have contested custody motions to a court service provider for the sole intent of increasing the non-primary parent's custody. The primary parent is not informed of the appointees motive. They cannot refuse to participate since failure to abide results in legal sanctions.

Section 3, AV Services to High-Conflict Families (pages 25-36), introduces psycho-education as a means to solve severe parenting faults like domestic violence, child abuse, alcoholism, drug abuse, criminal behavior, and non-existent parenting.

Parenting Coordinators (PC), described as "parents for the parents," are introduced as the court appointee meant to solve disputes and enforce the court custody order. PCs try to teach parents appropriate behavior by modeling it for them. After a brief meeting, parents can telephone or page the PC to referee clashes. Fees, in 2001, were $80 to $125 per hour.

> *Interventions to Provide Families With Parenting Conflicts with Long-Term Assistance*, pages 28, 29.

> "*Court orders and mediation agreements do not effectively end conflict for some couples with entrenched disputes, a history of litigation, and other dysfunctions. Several courts are experimenting with ways of providing more sustained forms of assistance with problem solving. They also hope that longer term intervention will help parents to learn more effective ways of parenting and practice implementing their court orders dealing with custody and visitation. These interventions are meant for "frequent fliers" in the court system.*"

Working with High Conflict Families admits severe character traits exist that would make co-parenting not only impossible, but dangerous. Yet the research relied upon to solve this dilemma is generated by AFCC affiliates and disseminated in its newsletter, Family and Conciliation Court Review (later changed to "Family Court Review"). The promising practice is a way for industry insiders to gain enormous profits from contested custody litigation.

Section 4, Services for Incarcerated Parents, pages 37-53, shows us that, under this federal program, criminal men are more suited for custody than full-time mothers. Ironically, men imprisoned for physical and sexual assault against their partner or child, are deemed rehabilitated. Mothers are court-ordered to bring children to prison visits. Support is waived. Short-term supervised visits may be ordered with eventual mediation and unsupervised custody awards.

Section 5 Services to Enforce Visitation, pages 55-68, illuminates another common practice: the use of legal assistance for dads to increase custody. Help with pro se filings, legal services, and ex-parte intervention (pages 60, 61, 64, 65), are cited as remedies to provoke a judicial contempt order against mothers. Three of the four research citations for this section were authored by Pearson.

"**Among sanctions available for contempt are fines, jail time, and a change of custody**" (page 62) has become the program standard for mothers who fail to comply, even when they have legitimate evidence of father's unfitness and harm.

Section 6, Working with Faith-Based Organizations, pages 69-83, highlights the prevalent use of Catholic Charities to run supervised visits, mediation, and prison programs, regardless of its background in patriarchy and pedophilia.

Another common practice is hidden in this section on working with ideologues: give the AV grant directly to family court administrative units. Page 77 confirms *"In Pennsylvania, the AV grant is given directly to the support office."*

Court services are fee-driven. Low-income dads do not possess the means to sustain extended consumption. *Promising Practices* recommends ways courts can facilitate usage. *"In Hawaii, fathers can work off their supervised visit fees by doing landscaping and remodeling the recreation room (page 71)."*

#2 - Strategic Planning Guide – The Conduit Document[10]

While *Promising Practices* offers sample programs, *Strategic Planning Guide* offers implementation. It gives permission. *Promising Practices* details specifics; *Strategic Planning Guide* is a

---

[10] Strategic Planning Guide: "A Collaboration and Strategic Planning Guide for States: Child Access and Visitation Programs," Pearson, 2006.

how-to. How to institutionalize the fatherhood mandate using key players: judges, support employees, legal and mental health court appointees. How to obtain input from those who have a stake in the program such as fatherhood advocates (page 12). The two reports are used in conjunction to market AFCC's commandeering of family court legal process.

NFI's founder, ACF's Assistant Secretary Wade Horn could easily leave his government position, join the Deloitte Consulting group's social services division and "sell" the fatherhood mandate as officially endorsed. Another government insider, Ron Haskins, could use his new position at Brookings Institute, and as a Casey Foundation board member, to fund and market these strategies. In fact, during the 2007 AFCC conference Haskins presented "Children, Marriage, Separation and Divorce: The Politics of Policy, Practice and Parenting" a workshop designed to "promote marriage values in the child support program," in conjunction with Institute for American Values staff Elizabeth Marquardt and court mediation promoter Robert Emery.

The fatherhood field premise that men who maintain custody are more likely to pay support arises on page 26. Missing is the algebraic formulation that increasing custody reduces support as a matter of course. Oddly (or not), mothers have identified the frequent occurrence of support offices permitting support arrears to accumulate, switching custody, thereby obliterating dad's support obligation, yielding payment-in-full.

Strategic Planning Guide gives the go-ahead for states to design their own protocols. It is the **conduit document** that allows trade group and father's rights groups to implement their agenda of using appointees and profiteers to cover-up abuse, and manufacture charges against mothers, including psychological labeling (alienation, mentally ill). In Pennsylvania, the follow-up document is called "*Changing the Culture of Custody in Pennsylvania.*"[11] The plan is available on Pennsylvania's bar website. The plan outlines the use of appointees to referee contested custody. Connecticut's *Strategic Planning Guide* is contained in their court administrative rules - the "Practice Book." Both guides were written by members of AFCC. Industry insiders enact *Strategic Planning Guide* differently in every state, using a variety of legislative and court administrative tools such as rules committees, commission reports, and task forces. In a 2015 AFCC published article *"Establishing Parenting Time in Child Support Cases: New Opportunities and Challenges"*[12] Pearson notes the strategy *"visitation can be implemented at the state level with legislation or the local/county level with local court rules."*

Strategic Planning Guide and its offspring, prove family courts single-handedly replaced judicial adjudication of custody - adhering to rules of evidence, fact and law - with an administrative mandate to relegate to court appointees under the guise of increasing father's access and visitation. As in *Promising Practices*, every page contains purposeful ignoring of due process, ethical standards and outright overriding of legislative laws written to protect women and children from all forms of maltreatment.

It is of note that current federal OCSE employee, Michael Hayes, is included in *Strategic Planning Guide* in his capacity of Manager of Collaborations, Fatherhood and Family Initiatives, Child Support Division, Office of Texas Attorney General.

Changing the Culture of Custody in Pennsylvania

I am providing evidence and commentary on implementation of *Strategic Planning Guide* within Pennsylvania. Around 2004,

[11] Changing the Culture of Custody in Pennsylvania: https://www.pabar.org/public/committees/CJI/Changing%20the%20Culture%20of%20Custody%20Committee%20Report%20and%20Recommendation.pdf
[12] "Establishing Parenting Time in Child Support Cases: New Opportunities and Challenges:" Pearson, 2015, Family Court Review, Vol 53, No. 2, pages 246-57

Pennsylvania convened the Judicial Initiatives Commission. A custody sub-group included numerous family court special interests – judges, lawyers, domestic violence, father's rights members, and AFCC mediation operative Shienvold, a participant in the 2013 fatherhood DV roundtable. The result, *"Changing the Culture of Custody in Pennsylvania,"* was based on practices being used in Connecticut, whose court has heavy AFCC infiltration. The culture that needed changing was contested custody. The plan decreed parents will be assigned court services (appointees) under the guise of making parent's cooperate and conciliate (mediation). Cases with high levels of contested custody will command abundant, court-ordered, fee-driven services. Any parent petitioning the other parent's unfitness – a parent who leaves a partner who cannot negotiate – who uses all means at their disposal to demand their way – who ignores routine child care needs – would be sent to a third party to decide custody concerns. The Plan has no exception for cases containing financial imbalances - such as when mother is a full-time caregiver and dad controls the family income. The gold-standard lauded in the Plan is appointment itself; **not** high adherence to ethical standards - Pennsylvania passed legislation denying parents a right to file ethical complaints against appointees. Even though Pennsylvania's domestic violence coalition (PCADV) staff were members of the commission, *Triage Intake Screen* (see below) was made the sole method of protection from abuse, irrespective of a statutory requirement to consider abuse a detriment in custody awards. DV staff did not point out flaws in the research or screen itself. Nor did those staff remind participants of a statute that prohibits counseling where there is evidence of domestic violence.

A subsequent legislative hearing included several father's rights groups given ample time to speak (15-30 minutes each). Mitch McConnell, head of the father's rights group ACFC, members of PA Fathers and Children Equality, and Fathers 4 Justice, participated in a working group to implement the Plan. PCADV spoke, yet made no reference to the existence of father's rights groups' participation in the working group or the hearing. PCADV did not apprise legislators of the nefarious nature of the father's rights agenda and their network of court appointees. Ironically, OCSE staff Michael Hayes, insists the collaboration between DV groups and *Strategic Planning Guide* implementers is sufficient protection against further abuse.

#3 - Jurisdictional Profiles and AV Guidance Reporting[13]

OCSE AV federal reporting form *"State Child Access Program Survey Guidance,"* (page 4, Counselors) requires **increasing** custody without consideration of sexual abuse of child(ren), physical violence, psychological abuse, coercive control, alcohol abuse, drug abuse, criminal history, and other negative or detrimental behaviors of the parent. Debra Pontisso is listed as the OCSE contact person on one form. Tracie Pogue is the contact for a duplicate form found on Oregon's website. A more recent reporting form admonishes counselors to focus solely on increasing custody and not alcoholism, drug addiction, anger, domestic violence, and "general" concerns such as child sexual abuse. Yet, these behaviors are important factors to be considered when awarding custody. Simply put – this one document solely proves the program mandates states to override legislative law which requires judges to factor-in abuse in determining custody.

The fact that the federal government is instructing counselors to ignore sexual abuse of a child may seem alarming in itself. However, the AV survey was produced for the purpose of reporting statistics of the increases achieved by these methods. The statistics are contained in *Jurisdictional Profiles* published

---
[13] Jurisdictional Profiles & AV Guidance Survey posted at http://www.maccabuse.org/research.php

yearly. This author has copies for the years of 2005, 2007, 2008 and 2013.

Yearly *Jurisdictional Profiles* prove family court and its appointees are singling out cases for intentional increases of custody through the use of "services." Some increases are awarded through supervised visits. In 2008, California reports using its nearly $1 million grant to increase custody for 1,577 parents, relying on supervised visits and parent education. (California refers cases to mediation in as little as ten visits according to an *"Access to Visitation Program Report to Legislators"* – see Ancillary documents below for details.) In 2013, California used its nearly $1 million grant to fund 1,000 supervised visits, 130 neutral drop-offs and 66 parent education. California reports increasing 434 father's and 179 mother's custody. California is known to label mothers who petition the court with claims of father's sexual abuse of the child as "alienators," award dads sole custody, require mothers to attend supervised visits - often for years and at great financial expense - until the children are re-programmed and sexual abuse ceases to be raised in litigation. Supervised visits in California are a way to condition mothers to accept shared parenting. So while the reporting favors dads, the truth is actually more nefarious, as mothers are sent to supervised visits for punishment, while fathers are sent for actual dangerous behavior.

Contrary to California's low number of parents reported to be helped under the AV grant, Texas's 2008 accounting claims 27,778 parents were served under its $886,000 grant. In 2013, the only year that includes a gender breakdown, Texas increased 5,201 father's custody through education, mediation, counseling, and custody orders and 856 moms. In 2013, Texas reports zero supervised visits as the method of increasing custody. Most likely, Texas obtained a separate funding stream such as OVW's Safe Haven grant. In 2011, Texas reported transferring $7.6 million from TANF to fund "formation of 2 parent families" (marriage/fatherhood programs).

Jurisdictional Profiles and the *AV reporting survey guide* raise serious questions. The numbers prove courts are selecting cases for increases of custody. Who determines what cases deserve increases? What are the parameters? Is the other parent informed that they are going to receive a custody decrease? What are the legal methods used to achieve the increases/decreases of custody? OCSE staff Michael Hayes has refused to respond.

OCSE pretends AV services are for low-income parents. However, the high cost of mediation, counseling, supervised visits and other services negates that claim. Fees are paid by parents. Any appointee can operate under the "mediation" label. Lawyers appointed to act on behalf of the child charge upwards of $600 per hour. Counselors and co-parenting coordinators bill $200 and above. Supervised visits start at $75/hr. Even average income parents could not sustain these fees for long. The claim that AV services exist for low-income parents is absurd. Additionally, it is unconstitutional to run two separate methods of custody determination – one for the poor and one for others. Ironically, two systems do exist in family court – one uses third-party, for-profit decision-makers and the other uses Child Protective Services to provide evidence to back-up changes of custody.

Connecticut's Fatherhood Initiative – connecting court services to fatherhood programs

Activists filed a Freedom of Information Act (FOIA) request for disclosure of access/visitation contracts. Retrieved agreements between the Department of Social Services and the Judicial Branch show the AV program operates to *"provide court referrals for conflict management services to chronically conflicted divorced or separated parents, relationship establishment counseling and supervised visitation and counseling for children of chronically conflicted parents."*

These contracts show AV services are given to "high conflict" families - those with contested custody. Activists were told litigants names are confidential. Connecticut activists have documented a pattern of severe cover-up of child sexual abuse and other parental misbehaviors by judges and court appointees. Connecticut, a state with a small population and therefore a small AV grant, has documented over 82 cases of severe denial of due process in order to award sole custody to highly abusive, wealthy, parents.

Connecticut transfers $22 million yearly from TANF to the John S. Martinez Fatherhood Initiative[14] – called the "lead" agency.

Under "resources" Martinez's website refers fathers to father's rights groups CRC and ACFC. The following question and answers show connections between various state agencies that give men preferential treatment (retrieved March, 2016).

> *What is the John S. Martinez Fatherhood Initiative of Connecticut?*
>
> *A: The John S. Martinez Fatherhood Initiative of Connecticut is a broad-based, multi-agency, statewide program led by the Department of Social Services that is focused on changing the systems that can improve fathers' ability to be fully and positively involved in the lives of their children.*
>
> *Q: What's the goal of the Fatherhood Initiative?*
>
> *A: The goal of the Fatherhood Initiative is to promote the positive involvement and interactions of fathers with their children by providing dads with the skills and supports they need to stay connected to their children.*

---

[14] http://www.ct.gov/fatherhood/site/default.asp

Q: When did the Fatherhood Initiative begin?

A: Fatherhood Initiative legislation was passed with bipartisan support in the fall of 1999, after state and local leaders continued to see children who had been affected by father-absence.

Q: Who is involved in the Fatherhood Initiative?

A: Partners in the Initiative include the Departments of Children & Families, Correction, Education, Labor, Mental Health & Addiction Services, and Public Health; Judicial Branch Support Enforcement Services and Court Support Services Divisions; CT Commission on Children; CT Coalition Against Domestic Violence; Legal Aid Services and numerous community-based partners serving families (mothers, fathers, and children).

TRADE ASSOCIATION PUBLICATIONS

Two premier Association of Family and Conciliation Courts (AFCC) publications provide ample background and protocol data to elucidate us about the intentional disregard for due process protections. Both documents were written by AFCC's Executive Director, Peter Salem. Salem holds degrees in political science, media and marketing. He is not a lawyer. Salem appears unqualified to author family court protocols; his training is best suited for the profession of lobbyist.

AFCC's sole purpose is to grow business for court appointees using the premise of mediation and shared parenting. If state law requires abuse to be viewed a detriment to custody, that protection is overridden by legal and mental health practitioners.

#4 - **Triage Intake Screen**[15]

---

[15] Triage Intake Screen: "Triaging Family Court Services: The Connecticut

Triage Intake Screen is the fatherhood program protocol for managing domestic violence. *Triage Intake Screen* treats abuse as a family dispute that needs to be resolved. Parents with dissolved or dissolving relationships, who file litigation, have histories of physical abuse, substance abuse, and/or concerns that the other parent is unfit, are rated as having varying levels of "conflict." The greater the protective parent perceives the abuser as a detriment to a healthy and safe home environment, the higher the court rates the level of conflict.

Triage Intake Screen minimizes the cause and risk factors of abuse. It merely measures parents' ability to communicate, cooperate and agree. *Triage Intake Screen* terms abuse a "family dispute." It rates those resistant to parenting alongside an abusive and unfit ex-partner, as a problem in calculating family dispute. By relegating maltreatment to a non-issue in custody determinations, evidence of harm, which would legally deem a parent unfit for custody, is suppressed. By ordering a third-party the court squelches proof - only the evaluator is permitted to submit evidence. A parent who has taken a sexually violated child to a medical doctor and confirmed anal penetration is not permitted to submit that evidence in court. An appointee is the only one allowed to decide if it is harmful to a child to be alone with the molesting father.

Obliterating Cause and Ethical Standards

Triage Intake Screen begins with a historical look at judicial assessment tools. Traditionally, non-legal, mental health trained appointees were used in an information-gathering capacity by judges assumed to be "too busy" to conduct in-depth judicial hearings and trials over contested custody litigation. As most contested custody litigation originated at the time of divorce or separation, the cause of the dissolution was a primary component

---

Judicial Branch's Family Civil Intake Screen", Salem, Kulak, Deutsch 2007
http://digitalcommons.pace.edu/cgi/viewcontent.cgi?article=1140&context=plr

of custody evaluations. However, courts have turned away from the "cause" of divorce breakup and *"custody evaluations that emphasized the identification of parenting abilities and assessment of primary parent-child relationships"* (page 4). Doing so permits courts and appointees to discount abuse and other behaviors that negatively impact parenting, and conversely, behaviors that positively influence parenting.

The American Psychological Association created guidelines for custody evaluations which include verifying facts (evidence) by way of collateral witnesses and assessment of parenting ability and the parent/child "fit." Adherence to these accepted guidelines is deemed ethical. Stepping outside of the industry standard is unethical. However, *Triage Intake Screen* bases parenting ability solely on whether parents can cooperate and communicate.

> *"This proliferation of dispute resolution processes has resulted in an exciting range of opportunities for service providers and users alike. What has not developed alongside these services is a clear set of criteria to help determine the optimal fit between clients and the services that best meet their needs."* (page 6)

The industry sees contested custody as an opportunity for service providers to profit from the problems of others - contention and abuse generate profits. *"Research indicates that a majority of couples succeed in moving beyond the anger, conflict and depression associated with divorce within two to three years following separation, as many as 1/3rd of divorcing couples report significant conflict over children many years later"* (page 6). While viewing these cases as opportunity, the authors express concern *"these cases often lead to burnout and stress among court counselors* (page 8)."

<u>Coaching</u>

Triage Intake Screen concedes litigants may have been coached. *"Political interests often gender related, surface. Prompted by organizations or books that provide guidance to separating and divorcing couples that may produce (conflict) rather than help resolve conflict. These include groups representing fathers' rights, victim advocates and mothers without custody"* (page 7). Victim advocates, presumed to represent abused women and children, are characterized as creating conflict instead of offering protection. Meanwhile, fathers' rights groups are equated with groups that protect women from abuse. The mention of "mothers without custody" could stem from protective parent organizations such as the Leadership Counsel, who educate the public on the use of Parental Alienation Syndrome (PAS) as a tactic to evade evidence of father's sexual abuse of the child. Ironically, AFCC does not refer to itself and its members as a political interest group.

Issue-focused/Hybrid Evaluations

Triage Intake Screen replaces standard court service progression. Instead of starting with a basic parent education class (level 1), cases deemed high conflict would go right to level 3, Parent Coordination. Instead of a traditional custody evaluation based on accepted APA guidelines, the screen permits "issue-focused" evaluations. AFCC terms issue-focused evaluations "hybrid" services, since evaluators combine dispute resolution with evaluation, creating a fertile field for overlooking abuse. For example, if there is child sexual abuse a court appointee would be assigned to determine the validity and/or encourage the parent resistant to the abuser having custody to cooperate and resolve the dispute. The emphasis is not on protecting the child from further harm but rather, continuing access for the abuser.

A distortion of traditional court services was already underway even before the institutionalization of *Triage Intake Screen*. *"Mediators altered the process to incorporate an information-gathering function, including GALS (court appointed child's attorney), information from other sources [not defined], and the mediator's own expertise. [This] enabled counselors to use their clinical judgment to reach agreement replacing custody evaluation"* (page 13).

Family Relations Counselors

Triage Intake Screen is administered by court employees called Family Relations Counselors. *"The counselor can be more directive than a mediator, can obtain collateral information and make recommendations... attorneys and GALs may be instrumental."* If no agreement is reached a report is sent to the court. The counselor can court order an issue-focused evaluation (page 14) (i.e. determine if sexual abuse of child, substance abuse, occurred/occurs.) *"Family relations counselors facilitate negotiations and provide information on child development, child custody, access and parenting matters, child support, property division and other financial matters."* They are court employees acting as mid-level judges. Other states may employ them under job descriptions of hearing masters/officers (Pennsylvania) or states attorneys (Texas).

In developing this new method of processing contested custody cases *"it became evident that the long history of cooperation between the bench [judges] and the bar [lawyers] and the high regard for Family Services Unit staff [court employees] would be key factors in the success of the project"* (page 14).

Salem acknowledges that *Triage Intake Screen*, could be self-administered. Instead the Family Relations Counselor completes the form. *"it was determined that counselors would be enabled to observe nonverbal communication clarify and probe using follow-up questions and employ their considerable clinical experience and judgment"* (pages 21-22). In actuality, third-party assessors are likely to manipulate outcomes and skew results because of personal bias, gender favoritism, fatherhood and father's rights training.

<u>The Screen Itself</u>

New litigation and divorce are rated "low conflict" while never married and living apart is rated "high conflict." The more the court is relied upon, and the higher in service progression, the higher the level of "conflict" (page 30 – Level of Conflict). At no point is the level of abuse to the other parent or children rated or deemed a cause for divorce and contested custody.

Assessing "Ability to Cooperate/Communicate" (page 31), stems from ideology promoted by Janet Johnston's domestic violence writings. *"Those who make unilateral decisions without reference to the other parent and those who do not see the value of the other parent to the children are less likely to settle in mediation"* (Johnston 1999). *Triage Intake Screen* does not measure communication and cooperation during the relationship, prior to litigation. It does not assess if one parent has historically been responsible for the majority of parenting duties. *"Self-reported inability to communicate and cooperate is strongly related to resistance to settlement in mediation and a need for more directive services"* (Johnston and Pearson). Triage Intake Screen does not assess if failure to communicate and cooperate are the cause of the relationship dissolution, thereby the screen invalidates a difficult, personal decision.

The Family Relations Counselor is asked to rate the "Complexity of Issues." Moving out of the jurisdiction is rated "high conflict" while *"appropriate daily care and discipline of your children"* is rated "low conflict" (page 31). This prioritizes a parent's physical presence over quality of care.

Page 32 assesses child abuse, substance abuse and mental health.

If these behaviors occurred in the past, they obtain a "low" rating. The rating increases based on the parents' level of denial. Thus, if a parent committed child abuse, yet admits it, the conflict is rated "moderate" as opposed to "high" for those denying the charge. Rating abuse as a "past" event fails to consider the potential for future abuse which could be enormously high. Rating level of admission is also extremely questionable, as it appears an abuser is encouraged to admit his abuse and it will be overlooked or deemed "cured." Rating mental health is also suspect in that mental health diagnosis are routinely given to mothers and children who have been the targets of the abuse; denial of a mental health diagnosis is appropriate in circumstances where the diagnosis is merely a legal strategy.

Rating domestic violence (page 33) holds the same problems in that, its severity is conditional on time period and level of denial. Incidents of domestic violence are solely validated by police reports, criminal prosecutions and orders of protection.

"Level of Dangerousness" is rated by level of fear against self, not the children. That means the screen rates whether a parent is afraid they will be harmed and not if a parent is afraid the other parent will harm the child(ren). Details of incidents of physical abuse and threats of physical harm are rated as low if they occurred in the past and infrequently. Ratings are applicable only to incidents against the parent, not the child (page 34). The form does not assess whether the fear is warranted by current and past behavior of the abusive parent.

Triage Intake Screen concludes with the Family Relations Counselor adding up the components and ordering court services. Those who harbor legitimate concerns are likely to be assigned comprehensive court services. The more abuse the greater the amount of court interference.

#5 - High Conflict Parent Education[16]

This National Institute of Health article, posted on the Health and Human Services website, gives the history of the replacement of judicial adjudication (due process) with third-party appointees. Services such as parent education, mediation, child custody evaluation, parenting coordination arose in order to get parents to mediate, resolve their dispute, co-parent. AFCC conferences and membership established networks and developed a market for parent education practitioners, administrators and researchers; supported legislative initiatives (fatherhood funding); and, developed program materials. The mediation network grew with Office of Child Support Enforcement (OCSE) access/visitation endorsement.

Although Salem admits *"It is inadvisable to think parent education will create long-term behavior change, heal the emotional scars of divorce, clear crowded court dockets or settle custody disputes without solid empirical evidence"* (Salem, 1996), access/visitation programs are designed to do just that: force abusive and negative behavior change solely by increasing custody.

> *"As with other family court practices like mediation and collaborative law, there exists no coherence in goals, priorities, practices and evaluation of parent education programs (Folberg, Milne, & Salem, 2004; Webb & Ousky, 2011). There is no convincing evidence that parent education reduces inter-parental conflict, enhances parent-child relationships or improves children's post-divorce adjustment."*
>
> *"Lawyers, judges, social workers, counselors, psychologists, mediators and social science research have all been involved in parent education program development, each of them having different goals, experience, knowledge and*

---

[16] High Conflict Parent Education: "Taking Stock of Parent Education in the Family Courts: Envisioning a Public Health Model" by Peter Salem (AFCC President), Irwin Sandler, Sharlene Wolchik, http://www.ncbi.nlm.nih.gov/pmc/articles/PMC3638966/

intent."

California is regarded as first and foremost in court mandated mediation, termed parent education. AFCC originated in California.

From this article we learn there are three (3) levels of parent education funded under AV grants. Level 1 is a traditional, several hour class. Level 2 is more intensive - designed to enhance co-parenting and conflict resolution. Level 3, given to high-conflict parents, is designed to reduce interparental conflict. Level 3 programs are described as experiential (learning by experience) and involve lengthy and multiple sessions. Level 3 parenting education is for women who report (and have evidence of) serious concerns about fathers' fitness and safety. This juxtaposition results in sessions where real concerns are discounted and ignored in order to force co-parenting. Concerns about safety and detrimental parenting are problematic obstacles.

Salem writes that **"divorce must be treated as a public health issue."** Treating divorce as a public health issue would make parenting education (and other court services) eligible for reimbursement under the Affordable Care Act. AFCC promotes judicial orders to mental health practitioners (MHPs) who then bill health care providers. Currently, MHPs must submit a diagnostic code for parents and/or children in order to be reimbursed for sessions. Classifying divorce as a public health issue will negate that requirement. Currently, MHPs use inappropriate diagnostic codes in order to receive reimbursement. For example, Connecticut activists documented MHPs inform the court that a child or mother suffers from PAS then bill using the code for bi-polar and oppositional defiant disorder.

After making a case for classifying divorce as a public health issue, Salem redefines the three levels of parent education. Each level acts as a substitute for due process. Services are mandated and parents are required to pay the practitioner.

Level 1 - Universal – informational – lowest level of denial of due process. Level 1 programs are *informational* in nature and promote better parental decision-making regarding legal and dispute resolution processes that may impact children's well-being.

Level 2 – Selected – moderate denial of due process – uses pressure (coercion) to jointly resolve legal issues. Level 2 services *"focus on skills for enhancing their children's post-divorce adjustment. Examples would be skill-building programs that teach effective discipline, effective co-parenting, methods for reducing inter-parental conflict and ways to handle common concerns such as communication around school or health-related issues."*

Level 3 – Indicated – severe denial of due process - the practitioner makes legal determinations in order to "save court resources." Level 3 services are *"designed for subgroups, such as high-conflict parents, and might aim to reduce interparental conflict. Level 3 programs are primarily experiential and multiple sessions in length. Indicated services are appropriate for parents who are behaving in a way that the court deems to be harmful to their children's well-being. Such behaviors might include intimate partner violence or chronic high levels of inter-parental conflict, particularly conflict that puts the children in the middle or that involves repeated re-litigation over issues of parenting time, which leads to a lack of family stability."*

Each of the three levels is designed to force co-parenting; not to protect children from a parent's physical, psychological or sexual abuse and negative behaviors like alcoholism and drug addiction. The more a parent fears the other parent and insists on protecting the child by limiting contact, the more intensive will be the behavior modification education.

Salem states *"Indicated mandated parent education programs protect the well-being of children."* Salem solely defines a child's well-being as having both parents. Parental abuse and negative behaviors do not impact a child's well-being, and a father is preferable to a mother who denies dad "access" (the opportunity to inflict harm on their child).

Salem admits **"there are important due process considerations that are beyond the scope of this paper"** for indicated services designed to "change behaviors" such as reducing inter-parental conflict.

Salem suggests the three levels of parent education should be integrated with other court services as a public health model. The programs will operate alongside custody evaluation, mediation, co-parenting coordination and collaborative law.

It is noteworthy that Nancy Ver Steegh (author of domestic violence primers, and participant in AFCC's Wingspread Conference) reviewed a draft of Salem's paper.

Ancillary Document

The industry generates a profuse amount of literature. Outsiders, independent voices who could refute claims, are non-existent. The industry encompasses governments, universities and professional organizations. No one will stand-up to the avalanche of material generated to validate the scheme. I've honed my ability to analyze documents for relevant facts that illuminate on the existing structure. I've included assessments throughout this book. Below is a report that shows what type of men are being reformed and given increased custody via supervised visits.

CALIFORNIA ACCESS TO VISITATION REPORT TO LEGISLATORS

This report, a ten-year program review, purports to assess California's AV services which are (1) supervised visits; (2) group counseling; and (3) parent education. However, little is written about group counseling and parent education - the report concentrates on supervised visits.

In the introduction we see California relies on *Strategic Planning Guide* and *Promising Practices* for its framework. California relies on partnerships with courts, child support and public and community groups. *"Courts and subcontractors improve parents compliance with court orders, facilitate reunification, teach parents conflict resolution and communication skills for problem solving. Supervised visits are a bridge to "normalized" visitation (page 5)."*

Reasons for supervised visit referrals are domestic violence and substance abuse. *"Domestic violence was reported by 53% of those in mediation. Four out of ten families referred had a restraining order. 38% said the child witnessed the assault. 86% of families were in mediation because they had a concern about the other parent's safety (25%); child neglect (22%); domestic violence (21%); drug abuse (18%); and alcohol abuse (19%). Half of those in mediation reported child safety as an issue."* Clearly, cases ordered to mediation have severe parental fitness concerns, and, if courts were following state custody statutes, due process, these cases would be not "tagged" for increases of custody as they are under AV administrative protocol.

In fact, California's AV plan admits father's extreme lack of parenting ability. On page 34, a supervised visit staff explains *"father had no understanding of the needs of the baby (9 months) nor did he know how to hold the child, soothe her, or feed her properly. The first visits were stressful and caused trauma for both father and child"* and *"one father stood over his four-year-old trying to talk with him during the visit and the little boy just shrank away. The father did not know or understand how to talk and connect with the child. When I sat down in a little chair and suggested that dad sit down in a little chair so he could make eye contact and we spent time talking together with the little boy. So he started doing that and now he tells me that he is "doing better" with the eye thing."*

California's assessment of supervised visits mentions *"an exit protocol that requires a minimum of 10 visits (or exchanges) before the parent can request a referral to a court connected child custody mediation to develop a revised visitation and/or exchange schedule. The AV coordinator may also refer the case to mediation (page 28)."* One can conclude that supervised visit centers exist merely to "heal" abusive fathers in as little as ten visits. After these ten visits, mother is required to agree to unsupervised custody, whether or not she still has concerns for her safety or that of the child.

Page 30 mentions a *"collaboration between three family courts and community organizations that provides counseling and education designed to increase NCP custody. Education and therapeutic services are used to rectify past problems and prevent future conflict and to facilitate NCP custody."* Mothers will attest that few of the fathers stop their pattern of mistreatment.

In California 160,000 divorces are filed per year; 100,000 families receive mediation. Group counseling sessions are defined as any combination of mother, father, and/or children.

California relies on AFCC's high conflict parent education. Given these high numbers, given the nefarious nature of abuse, given the profit motive of court appointees – is it any wonder California is recognized as a state with an extreme crisis in famiy court?

Conclusion

By layering these five premier documents we gain a thorough picture of the deception. We learn the players orchestrating the scam. Each document portends to be innocuous. Yet, take in the entirety, learn the language, read within the lines, discover the deeper motive of control, manipulation and profit.

From jurisdictional profiles we learn:

1. <u>The federal government funds a custody mandate.</u>

    "42 U.S.C. 669b – PRWORA (welfare reform) – authorized access/visitation grants to enable states to establish and administer programs to support and facilitate noncustodial-parent access to and visitation of their children..."

2. <u>Taxpayer money goes directly to court administrative units.</u>

    "Money to State Courts – Grants funds are given to Administrative Offices of the Court and State Child Support Enforcement Agencies (Domestic Relations, Support Offices)"

3. <u>Instead of judicial adjudication, court appointees and service providers determine outcomes.</u>

    "Section 391 of P.L. 104-193 permits the use of "Court Service Providers" acting under interchangeable labels of (1) mediation; (2) counseling; (3) parent education (all levels); (4) development of parenting plans; (5) visitation enforcement; (6) monitored visitation; (7) neutral drop-off and pickup; (8) supervised visitation; (9) development of guidelines for visitation and custody.

    Source: *ACF/OCSE/Child Access and Visitation Grants: State/Jurisdiction Profiles for FY 2008*

CHAPTER FOUR

Domestic Violence v. Family Court

The general public has been sold the misconception that domestic violence (DV) supports mothers who leave abuse. This notion is a commonly accepted untruth. In actuality, The Office of Violence Against Women and its grantees adhere to welfare reform – fatherhood and marriage promotion. In this chapter I describe why and how.

Criminal v. Civil

DV groups classify abuse as physical violence. They operate under a Department of Justice (DOJ) umbrella. Family Court is not criminal court. Family court is civil court. It operates under HHS (Health and Human Services) not DOJ. HHS is social service not criminal prosecution. Under HHS is the Office of Child Support Enforcement funded by Social Security IV-D. Juvenile court, an arm of family court, operates Child Protection Services (CPS) funded by Social Security IV-B.

DV funding was put in place to expedite the criminalization of physical assault against a female partner. Historically, women were viewed as property of parents and then their husbands. Husbands were permitted to physically assault their wives. During the 1960's and 70's women's cries for equality led to society viewing male violence against female partners as wrong. Feminists called for criminal prosecution where previously local police and prosecutors overlooked these assaults. Law enforcement had to be trained to respond seriously when males committed domestic violence.

Law enforcement will not automatically criminally charge violent men. Instead, a preference for "Protection From Abuse orders" developed (also called: PFAs, Restraining Orders, Protection Orders). The orders require violent men to stay away from the victim. If they refuse, prosecution ensues. Society shifted from prosecuting assault to offering victims a semblance of protection via court orders of no contact.

Protection orders are limited in time and they do not automatically cover minor children and custody visits. For instance, a man is ordered to stay away from his wife, yet he is given unsupervised weekend and day visits with his children. Generally, the mother is ordered to conduct exchanges in a "safe" environment – public area, police station or a center paid-for with fatherhood and VAWA funds. If a man is deemed seriously dangerous, a mother may be ordered to bring the children to a supervised visit so the kids do not lose contact with their father. It is extremely rare for mothers to be given a protection order that eliminates father's interactions with their children altogether. To gain one, mothers have to file a PFA on behalf of the child. DV does not assist a mother seeking protection for her children. If father is physically or sexually abusive to his child, Child Protection Services (CPS) is funded to investigate and make a determination of safety with an ultimate goal of keeping contact between father and child.

DV is not funded to stop child abuse. Omitting children was a purposeful decision of early advocates. DV money merely offers a panacea - temporary respite – safety planning and 30-day out-of-primary residence sheltering. If a woman with minor children wants to terminate a shared residence relationship, DV does not assist. Her options are to file for a Protection Order which mandates that father leave the home; leave herself and stay with family or friends; take her children to a shelter that includes space for children; or flee, perhaps packing a car and driving to another state, an action that can result in kidnapping charges.

In truth, DV is funded to convince women that father's deserve access and visitation, or contact with their children, in keeping with Welfare Reform mandates. DV traditionally lobbied for supervised visits between dangerous men and child. DV funding includes money for centers called the Safe Haven's grant. The growth of protection orders led to a growth in supervised visit centers. However, most centers that receive government grants have little to no understanding of the factors that contribute to domestic violence. Moreover, a theory written by pro-male sociologist Janet Johnston, advanced by AFCC and fatherhood programs, has taken root within the DV industry - that violence is a learned behavior and can be unlearned in a relatively short period of time.

Litigation Is A Tactic of Abuse

Unlike family court, abusers cannot use criminal court to hold onto their prey. They cannot hire mental health and legal interlopers to submit opinions that get them off, or blame the harmed for having caused his outburst. Criminal court being under the Department of Justice, is beholden to the Rule of Law. That means judges must use established conventions for determining valid evidence and witness from fraud and hearsay.

But abusers can use family court litigation to continue their control; to harass, intimidate, isolate and harm. Because family court operates under HHS, it is not required to hold to high legal standards. Litigants are not given representation as in criminal court where the charged either pays for an attorney or is given a public defender, and the victim is spoken for by a member of the local prosecutor's office that concluded a crime has been committed.

Criminal court punishes vicious men. It shields the victim from further harm. Family court gives men power. It forces the victim into continuous interaction. Criminal court sees brutality as a crime. Family court (juvenile, support and custody) exist to foster relationships between malicious dads and their children. Violence is curable. Incest is not a criminal offense. Father's sexual molestation is managed by CPS whose ultimate goal is keeping the parent/child connection.

In family court, children do not have the right to live away from incest, physical assault, mental degradation, or neglect if the perpetrator is their father. Mother's do not have the right to demand the child be protected. Children are property and in contested custody situations, fathers are superior property owners to mothers.

Cognizance of a victim (vic) and perpetrator (perp) is another difference between criminal and family court. The vic has been harmed by a specific act committed by the perp. The perp is the defendant. The plaintiff is the government. The victim does not litigate against her attacker. In family court, one parent is the defendant and the other is the plaintiff. In contested custody each party requesting primary custody files as a plaintiff and names the other party as the defendant. An abused mother is alone in a sea of professionals, overwhelmed by the magnitude of having to fend for herself.

In criminal court the victim is deemed helpless. She cannot retaliate or enact justice alone. A victim is sheltered by the system, treated as someone deserving protection. Family court is not a vic/perp relationship. It is personal – two people interacting. In family court, a mother leaving an oppressive situation or testifying to father's acts of vehemence is subject to derision and shame. Victims are accused of making it up to gain an advantage – **they** deserve punishment – **not** the offender.

Verb Victim v. Noun Victim

There are two types of victim. The noun victim is merely a subject or target. The harm they are subjected to has little influence over their demeanor. They adjust and figure out how to live well within the constraints of life with an abuser. The noun victim is strong. They have methods to shield their emotional pain. They put barriers between their actions and their distress. You may know a noun victim. They hold themselves with an attitude of "don't mess with me." They do not melt if not offered protection. They know what is best for themselves. The noun victim is a foreign entity to DV staff. She is not likeable because she is not meek. She is angry at systemic mistreatment. She is more likely to be classified "mutually abusive" or "situational couples violence" because she may have used force to protect herself.

The verb victim emotes. They cry, tremble and have difficulty moving beyond what is or has caused them pain. They become lost in a sea of mistreatment. They feel helpless and unable to stop or minimize the behavior of the person who is persecuting them. They look to others for rescue. They are reliant on others for protection. DV staff encourage the verb victim. DV staff portray all subjects of abuse as verb victims, unable to comprehend and solve their situation. The image of a women crying in a corner with hands over her face while he threatens her with his fists is the most comfortable portrayal of an abusive relationship to DV staff.

Since only the most egregious assaults have criminal trials, where the victim is required to testify, DV staff who come into contact with abused women through victim advocacy, interact and observe the most vulnerable victims, those who are forced to relive the event in order to portray it at trial. DV staff come into contact with the most susceptible victims thru shelters. Shelters house women who are out-of-sorts, who fled at a moment's notice, left homes and possessions, family, friends and routines. Counseling sessions offered at DV centers detail the trauma rather than the methods of survival standard within most abusive homes.

This interface results in a fallacy perpetuated by DV staff that mothers behave in ways that cause family court to rule against them. They act nervous. They contradict their stories. They emote. They are hysterical. They exaggerate. They lie. They hate men. They are vindictive. They are incapable of speaking for themselves, telling their own stories in clear, concise sentences. Their behavior and mannerisms have caused family court to label them mentally deranged, even deserving of his mistreatment.

Victim as Noun

Contrary to the stereotypical DV victim, mothers who enter divorce court and support offices have decided to leave, they have taken the first step towards recovery. They are not timid and cowardly. They do not act "crazy." They act strong. They can be angry and become even angrier when they realize the court is mistreating them. They are afraid of the man they know to be a constant menace. They know his habits are insidious and nefarious. They become despondent because family court is structured to ignore these factors. Family court treats the plaintiff and defendant as equals – the matter to be resolved is a civil matter, not criminal.

The everyday strife that is an underlying part of an abusive relationship entails emotional harm and mental manipulation – acts that are not prosecutable crimes. Strangulation is difficult to prove in criminal court. A woman who has physically defended herself by digging her fingernails into his forearms, looks as if she is violent, whereas he has left no visible marks. A man hides toilet paper in order to make mom think she is imagining purchasing it. Does she cower and cry? No, she keeps the receipt in her handbag to confirm the purchase. She's learned to function within the abusive parameters set-up by dad. Other non-criminal acts like shaming, ridiculing, isolating, bullying and oppressing are prompters for mothers to file custody actions. The strong woman, the noun victim, has decided to stop a cycle of abuse - often because of the negative effects on her children and the fear that his bad behavior has been, and will be, directed towards the children. Because of his nature, these dads rarely contribute to child care duties so there is no history of how he will perform if given unsupervised custody. Mom positioned herself between dad and child in order to impede his harm. Mom kept a close eye on how he treated her kids. Mom and child had their own life away from his misbehavior, while he was at work or detached when at home.

Women with children develop defenses. Whether that means she stays in another room and plays with the kids, frequently visits her mother, or coaches them to be quiet and avoid dad when he is home. It is unfair to women who live with perpetual abuse to term them incompetent and label them as victim. Women live with male harassment in many forms throughout their lives. They learn to adjust. They become adept at avoiding harm. They have tools to protect their children until the day family court gives him unsupervised visitation or custody. They often present as competent and happy to mask the turmoil within their homes.

Abused mothers know father is unfit. That he does not parent. Does not nurture and caregive. He will now have unfettered access to the children whom mother has spent their lifetime protecting. These women know his mistreatment of the child is related to his mistreatment of her. His cruelty stems from his soul. They cannot fathom the inability of courts and DV groups to acknowledge their right to leave an abuser and expect the children to remain in her care.

Is DV Unaware?

In family court it is the way litigation ensues that creates the crime. Obfuscation, collusion, fraud, tampering with evidence, color-of-law violations deny parties their right to a fair hearing. An abused mother is quickly caught up in a plethora of tactics developed by father's rights and trade association members. Women with children beg local, state and federal DV groups to help because they understand that his abuse is the impetus for the avalanche of lies, coercion, punishment and threats occurring under the guise of litigation.

DV groups are fully aware that family court players know dad is highly dysfunctional. DV staff are unwilling to speak up and tell the public the truth – that their funding does not help women with minor children who want to cut-off connections with their abuser. Their structure is based on old norms of women remaining in the relationship. DV is afraid of losing their source of income which funds generous salaries, expense accounts, and research grants. DV staff are unwilling to disrupt their comfortable status. They are aligned with powerful men and not powerless mothers and children. They prop-up the male regime, where men remain on top and women and children remain secondary.

DV staff sell the illusion that abused women are bad mothers – that the abuse makes mom incapable of caring for her children. The children suffer because mom is physically bruised and mentally depressed or traumatized. She is not making healthy meals, can't get out of bed and pack school lunches. Is so isolated the children have no social life. Ironically, many mothers attend church, volunteer at school and sporting events, even while being viewed as worthless by dad.

In addition to treating moms as if they are continuously being beaten in front of the children, DV does not address the issue of father's treatment of the kids. Abuse of children is not a DV concern. This works out to be highly detrimental for mothers who leave because the abuser almost automatically turns his anger towards the children – they act as substitutes for her. Mom could protect the child while she was living with dad. When mom leaves and court gives him visits, mom can do nothing about his mistreatment besides raise the issue in family court. When that occurs mom is labeled an impediment to dad's relationship with his offspring. Yet this common occurrence is not funded by VAWA or OVW, nor will DV staff speak publicly about father's abuse of the legal system and children.

OVW Funded "Fathering After Violence"

In fact, OVW helps abusive men create a record of non-abuse to win custody. Dads who commit physical assault, who have been absent for long durations - often due to prison sentences - and dads who have molested the child, are given "step" visitation. They begin with supervised visits, frequently at a center funded by VAWA and OVW Safe Havens or Family Violence Prevention Fund grants. After several visits, dads are awarded unsupervised time. Mothers must mediate – agree to let dad have physical custody of the child – in as few as ten supervised visits. Mothers who refuse to give dad unfettered contact, face contempt charges.

Since the intent of court intervention is to change parents' behavior and force father's access, rather than to protect mothers and children, supervised visits for men are short-term affairs. It is mothers who become long-term consumers. Supervised visits are punishment used by the system to threaten and achieve silence. Mothers and children are told "you will have no relationship unless you keep quiet about father's abuse."

An OVW report entitled "Fathering After Violence: Working With Abusive Fathers in Supervised Visitation"[17] explains the disparity.

> *"in most centers some (if not many) parents ordered to visits) are mothers"* and *"some of whom might be in fact victims, rather than perpetrators of domestic violence."* (page 45)

> *"in some centers mothers make up almost half of the (supervised) visit caseload, this document was designed to target in particular visiting fathers who have been violent with their intimate partners."* (page 6)

Two themes are highlighted:

- violent men will change; and,

---

[17] "Fathering After Violence: Working With Abusive Fathers in Supervised Visitation" written by Juan Carlos Arean, 2007, with an Office of Violence Against Women's Family Violence Prevention Fund grant,

- mothers and children benefit from contact with their abuser.

"Giving abusive fathers (and all men) more opportunities for change and healing is an essential component of ending violence against women and children."

"Abuse is a learned behavior and deliberate choice and therefore can be unlearned."

"Centers show fathers the effects of witnessing and experiencing violence on children, and therefore create an impact that might persuade them to renounce their violence. Fathers are more easily to develop empathy towards their children than their partners (mothers) and this pathway to empathy can help some men reflect upon and change abusive and violent conduct."

"Men who use violence can be held accountable for their behavior and simultaneously be encouraged to change it; and women and children can benefit from this approach."

Even though this report lists key characteristics of abusers -- intimidation, psychological abuse, an inflated sense of self-entitlement, physical abuse, control, selfishness, superiority, possessiveness, confusion of love and abuse, externalization of responsibility, denial, minimization and victim blaming, and serial battering -- visitation staff are advised not to stereotype and over-generalize by assigning these characteristics to batterers under supervision. Typical traits identified by Bancroft and Silverman, experts in working with battering men, such as authoritarianism, under-involvement, neglect and irresponsibility, undermining of the mother's parenting and authority, self-centeredness, manipulativeness and ability to perform under observation are discounted when assessing for changed behavior.

Visitation centers are advised to establish a relationship with fatherhood programs (page 35). Some centers have fatherhood programs on-site. Curiously, the report states *"these programs are different from so-called "father's rights" groups and can offer expertise and materials on positive father engagement."* Yet, the report goes on to state *"most of these programs could also clearly benefit from receiving training to advance their understanding of domestic violence dynamics."*

The Office of Violence Against Women is telling supervised visit centers to refer violent men to fatherhood programs whose chief partnership is with courts to get men custody, all the while acknowledging that fatherhood programs know nothing about abuse and claiming those programs are not agents of male supremacy! It seems safe to conclude that the Family Violence Prevention Fund and OVW are promoting patriarchy; surely not helping battered mothers and children to leave abuse, but to encourage and force them into long-term shared parenting situations that ignore the vast array of non-physical harms. Mothers who resist will eventually find themselves court-ordered to supervised visits where their presence will be ignored by OVW grant funding.

Research on Violence

The research relied upon by the family court industry is selective and self-generated. It is funded by fatherhood grants, private conservative think tanks and endowments and the industry itself. It is disseminated in trade association newsletters and university journals which serve as the training ground for court appointees. Begun in the 1970s, the network created and relied upon a wealth of professionals to generate research that favored patriarchy; selective research is a common thread of father's rights and trade association members. Rather than moving forward an understanding of abuse – cause, implication, impact – men, and women who support the male regime, generated whitewashed stories that physical violence was a learned behavior and could be unlearned; that violence was sometimes warranted because women and children deserved it or challenged his authority; that no criminal conviction for one year meant he was reformed.

Judith Wallerstein was one such early advocate of the patriarchy viewpoint that children needed frequent contact with their fathers and mothers were to blame for a lack thereof. Her colleague, Janet Johnston,[18] currently promulgates bent ideology that males are necessary and, if violent, they can be rehabilitated by coaching them to "let go of baggage." The idea is rooted in a belief that a professional can tell men with long histories of violence, learned in father-violent homes, to let it go - instantaneously, violence is cured. The same thinking is used when incest is the misdeed – tell dad to stop and he will. Conversely, mothers are told to "let go of baggage" which is defined as past incidences of fathers violence and incest. If mom persists in petitioning for safety she is holding onto baggage and being a gatekeeper.

Janet Johnston is the creator of the domestic violence classification system explained in *"Motherless America: Confronting Welfare's Fatherhood Custody Program."* This system

---

[18] Janet Johnston: https://www.linkedin.com/in/janet-johnston-2b76b358/ "Janet R. Johnston Ph.D. is a professor emeritus from the Department of Justice Studies, San Jose State University. She was formerly a consulting associate professor at Stanford University and director of research for the Judith Wallerstein Center for the Family in Transition, in California and its affiliates. For three decades she specialized in counseling, mediation and research with high-conflict, litigating divorcing couples and their children with special attention to domestic violence, child abduction and alienated children. The social policy implications of research findings for family law, and how to develop multi-disciplinary partnerships with the court and a continuum of services within the community for divorcing families are special interests. She is the principal or sole author of more than 60 published papers, two books (Impasses of Divorce, 1988; In the Name of the Child, 2009 2nd Ed, a treatment manual (A Safe Place to Grow, 2005) and a book of therapeutic stories for children (Through the Eyes of Children, 1997). Over the course of her career, she has presented at hundreds of scientific and professional meetings for mental health professionals, attorneys, judges, and court administrators throughout the USA, Canada, Australia and Europe and been the recipient of numerous prestigious awards for her contribution to the field."

minimizes father's responsibility and classifies many instances of violence as being caused by circumstance or the victim themself. Lundy Bancroft refuted Johnston's classification dynamic as early as 1998 – yet, to date, the premise is still a foundation of family court policy.

A typical tactic of the network when one of their systems has been ousted is to bury and reincarnate it under a different name. Janet Johnston's classification was rewritten by Michael Johnson, consequently re-written by Nancy Ver Steegh, an AFCC President and BWJP affiliate. Ver Steegh's rewritten Johnston classification system was henceforth taken to Wingspread Conference, a joint meeting between the trade association, judicial ethics group and domestic violence group (AFCC, NCJFCJ, BWJP) funded by the Annie E. Casey Foundation. Wingspread attendees concluded that co-parenting coordinators should be assigned in all contested custody cases. Wingspread is an example of "collaboration" touted by OCSE staff Michael Hayes. Instead of requiring strict oversight and accountability, OCSE concludes encouraging special interests to work together will result in high adherence to law and ethical standards.

Is violence the singular indicator of harm?

What are an abused mother and children to do when confronted by an enormous industry intent on favoring males? No funding exists to question and refute research built on a premise of male superiority. An enormous machine with tentacles in government, non-profits and universities has had decades to forward its male domination agenda. Even when their premise is called into question, the industry has the ability to recirculate it under a new definition or venue.

Patriarchy-derided research is responsible for extreme custody outcomes – when severely harmful fathers are granted sole ownership of children. DV aids welfare reform programs grounded in male-superiority ideology. In addition to the administration of supervised visit centers, domestic violence staff work with Child Protection Services reunification programs. An article published in the New Haven Register entitled "Connecticut DCF finds success in domestic violence program for fathers"[19] recounts how severely abusive fathers are easily given full custody by participating in a short rehabilitation program. After less than six months in treatment, Wigberto 'George' Ortiz, a father with a history of violent reactions to stress, and admitted alcohol abuse, was given sole custody of four young children, two of whom have special needs. Fathers for Change relies on Johnston's misinformed belief that violence is a learned behavior and can easily change. In actuality, violence is often a means of asserting authority - male privilege. Violence - like litigation that demands sole custody - is used to intimidate, dominate, threaten and punish. A man who willingly takes his children from their mother, with whom they have developed a primary caregiver bond, is highly indicative of a male who will act inappropriately towards those same kids, especially when under duress. However, the probability of his harming his kids is ignored and not assessed by DV program staff, family court judge or the newspaper reporter. Neither did anyone note mothers side of this story.

Trumpian harm

Trumpian abusers suffer great amounts of psychological dysfunction. If violence exists it is coupled with large amounts of mental distortion. Change could only be possible by intensive immersion in a regimented system with identifiable outcomes. Cognitive behavior therapies have only recently gained influence – their use to change abusive behaviors could be negligible, and hasn't been scientifically studied to date, yet cognitive behavior therapy would seem to be more promising than the coaching currently being used in supervised visit and reunification programs, and certainly safer than using children as a vehicle for

[19] "Connecticut DCF finds success in domestic violence program for fathers" Hernandez, Esteban L., Aug.20,2017
http://www.nhregister.com/connecticut/article/Connecticut-DCF-finds-success-in-domestic-11945723.php

change.

Alternative Research

Knowledge of the cause, impact and implications of the multi-facets of male abuse is extremely limited since funding and research has been geared towards propping up a patriarchal system even within disbanded families. To analyze research - to determine if a pre-conceived outcome favorable to males exists - one should ask:

- "Who funds the research?"
- "Who generated the references relied upon to make new conclusions (requires a close inspection of footnotes)?"
- "Did a special interest group publish, and if so, does publication forward an agenda?"
- "Are the author's conclusions evidence-based? Science-based? Non-biased data-based?"

"Typologies of Male Batterers: Three Subtypes and the Differences Among Them" published in 1994,[20] scrutinize various studies of male batterers, most of whom were prosecuted for assault and/or referred for treatment. This study examines the male himself, and not the females' actions. Focusing on the women, what she did before and after the incident, her emotional state, creates a cover for male's behavior. That diversionary trick is common to researchers who use a baseline of male superiority – a foundation of family systems/dynamics theory. Unique to this study is that the authors do not question whether she provoked or deserved the violent attack. They look at why he behaved abusively.

By assessing numerous studies available at that point in time, the

---

[20] "Typologies of Male Batterers: Three Subtypes and the Differences Among Them" Holtzworth-Munroe, Stuart, Psychological Bulletin, Vol. 116(3), Nov. 1994, pp. 376-497.

authors concluded there are:

Three types of batterers:

1. <u>Family only</u> – the violence is directed within the family;
2. <u>General violent/antisocial</u> – the violence permeates his interactions and he exhibits additional socially inappropriate occurrences;
3. <u>Dysphoric/borderline</u> – the violence is related to an underlying psychopathology.

Three basic causes:

1. <u>Genetic</u> – violence is due to brain construction;
2. <u>Experience/learned in childhood</u> – violence is a learned response; and
3. <u>Peer accepted</u> – violence is accepted, even warranted, as a means of control by the social group.

Four risk factors:

1. <u>Attachment/dependence</u> – inappropriate amounts lead to violence when threatened.
2. <u>Impulsivity</u> – actions are controlled by three responses. The need for reward (behavior activation system); a fear of punishment (behavior inhibition system); and thrill/novelty-seeking.
3. <u>Social Skills</u> – inappropriate skills to respond to upsets and disagreements, a lack of an ability to resolve conflicts and problem-solve.
4. <u>Attitude</u> – a strong belief in woman's subjugated role; the belief in the right of male control of women; and the belief that violence is an acceptable means to assert authority.

Greater amounts of each cause and risk factors lead to a higher probability that violence will occur. The authors identify reward and punishment as deterrents.

Violence is not just a learned behavior. Even men with records of severe violence have numerous motives and triggers for their action. Reasons for commission are deep-seated. Abuse has scope. Abuse is psychologically driven. Abuse is a belief, a feeling of right and ownership. Abuse can be societally encouraged. Empowering abusers makes it increase. Penalizing may make it decrease.

Altering bad behavior which has a multitude of prompts is a complex matter. Real change is a long, tedious process that may never resolve itself. Shouldn't society show concern for those affected? Shouldn't women and children be permitted to leave, rebuild and have limited, controlled contact? Should children be a reward and an implement to effect change?

Women and children are severely harmed when family court special interests, including domestic violence staff, minimize the nature of abusive men. When policies limit the dynamic of why abuse occurs, how it is executed and when a culprit has reformed. Ironically, family court rewards abusive fathers by zealously forcing access.

Litigation: A Tactic of Abuse

We have all heard Donald Trump threaten to sue women who spoke out about his predatory behavior. He sues business associates, employees, anyone who doesn't fall in line. At one point he had 42 separate court actions occurring simultaneously. Litigation is a threat. Litigation is harassment. Litigation is a means to gain control - to subjugate - to condemn - to traumatize. Litigation is a dance that abusers enjoy orchestrating against their weary subjects.

The domestic violence community is well aware that custody and support litigation is a favored means of harm - that abusive men contest custody for several reasons including: to keep control, to retain a financial advantage, to punish. Research has existed through the 1990s and early 2000's,[21] yet custody awards to abusers have continued and grown while the advocacy movement has mostly remained silent or has spoken exclusively about cases with severe proof of child sexual molestation. A compendium of available research is easily accessible to family court industry insiders. Yet, knowledge of the vastness of the problem has had no effect in stopping growth.

Deciding custody when abuse exists

There have been federal legislative efforts geared at protecting abused parties from custody awards to abusers. In 1990, Congress passed House Consolidated Resolution 172 which deemed abuse to be a negative factor when making custody awards. Based on that viewpoint, The Model Code, developed by the National Council for Juvenile and Family Court Judges (NCJFCJ), states "it is considered detrimental to a child and not in his or her best interest to be placed in sole custody, joint legal custody or joint physical custody with an abusive parent." Thirty-seven (37) states have passed custody statutes that include consideration of abuse.

Twenty years ago, the proposed VAWA legislation included this passage:

> "According to a 1996 report by the American Psychological Association (APA), which Congress views as authoritative on matters of domestic violence and child custody and visitation determinations, custody and visitation disputes are more frequent when there is a history of domestic violence. Further, **fathers who batter mothers are twice as likely to seek sole custody of their children and they may misuse the legal system as a forum for continuing abuse through harassing and retaliatory legal actions.**"[22]

---

[21] "Are 'Good Enough' Parents Losing Custody To Abusive Ex-Partners?" Dallam, Stephanie, updated May 27, 2006
http://www.leadershipcouncil.org/1/pas/dv.html

Rather than mount a public relations effort to inform the public and government of the underpinnings of abuse when dads fight for custody, especially when those same men have seldom participated in childcare and household duties, domestic violence staff petition for funding to represent mothers in custody and support litigation. Instead of acting as a go-between for knowledgeable lawyers and abused mothers - as modest as maintaining a record of competent, affordable attorney's - domestic violence staff have stayed silent while the trade association and father's rights community forcefully network and expand their reach.

---

[22] https://www.scribd.com/document/96081543/VAWA-Title-2-The-Entire-MISSING-Section-of-the-VAWA-Identifying-Use-of-PAS-Legal-Strategies-as-Violence-Against-Women-Which-Endangers-Children

CHAPTER FIVE

Community Fatherhood v. Family Court Outcomes

Welfare Reform changed the war on poverty to promoting fatherhood and marriage – the conservative family values claim that women and children can avoid poverty by reliance on a man. A hidden agenda has always been male control – Patriarchy. Fatherhood and marriage promotion programs operate at the community level – prisons, churches, YMCA's. Disguised within the pages of fatherhood reports is the true nature of fatherhood – to generate family court outcomes in favor of dad regardless of behavior.

Reports tell us how fatherhood programs operate.

Strengthening Families Evidence Review (SFER)

"Catalog of Research: Programs for Low-Income Fathers" also known as "Strengthening Families Evidence Review" (SFER),[23] was written by Mathematica Policy Research in December 2011, for the Office of Planning Research and Evaluation, Administration of Children and Families. SFERs addresses community-level programs.

---

[23] "Catalog of Research: Programs for Low-Income Fathers" also known as "Strengthening Families Evidence Review" (SFER), was written by Mathematica Policy Research in December 2011

Access/Visitation

Court services run under the access/visitation (AV) label have limited review (pages 335-44). SFERs did not look at how courts operate these programs - merely if they successfully increased custody awards to fathers. AV services have no income limitations and SFER lists 50-75% as having income of $20,000 plus (page 337). 53-83% of those receiving AV services are defined as "white." 75% have training and education above high school. Unlike other fatherhood programs, AV, which operates the court appointee system, exist for well-to-do dads.

Chapter Three "Modus Operandi" details how access/visitation fatherhood programs supplant due process protections.

Fatherhood Programs Lack Evidence Review

SFERs contains few Impact Studies. SFER gave most fatherhood programs a low rating for adherence to scientific standards. Because of the low accountability, the authors of SFERs state *"the field lacks a body of rigorous research evidence and evidence-based program models. Of the more than 150 studies examined by SFER, only 7 received a rating of "high" for the quality of the methods and procedures used to determine program effectiveness."* Father's Rights and AFCC affiliate, Jessica Pearson, Social Policy Review, has been the contractor of record for most fatherhood program review.

A 17-page Research to Practice Brief entitled *"Using Documentation and Data in Fatherhood Programs"* written by SFER team members informs fatherhood programs of the need to collect, document, organize and analyze data. The brief is a primer showing the basics of scientific documentation standards with links to web videos and forms. The brief mentions that many fatherhood programs offer co-parenting. Analysis of abuse is not a suggested demographic. Negative behaviors such as crime, drug and alcohol use are mentioned, but it is stated that their presence may be more easily documented by "informal" chats, as opposed to structured questioning. Programs do not currently record fathers custody and support orders when they begin the program and when they end. The programs are not told to speak with mothers. It is noted that more intake questions may make men less likely to participate.

Mathematica staff were contracted to develop better program reviews. One such review, *"Responsible Fatherhood Programs in the Parents and Children Together (PACT) Evaluation,"*[24] was featured in AFCC's newsletter, Family Court Review. Addressing the family court audience - trade group members – the review points out that the federal government funds fatherhood programs in order to increase dads custody (called access, visitation or parenting-time). The PACT programs under review are gender-specific – for fathers - mothers are not participants nor are they interviewed.

Partners with Family Court

PACT evaluation introduces a common practice: fatherhood programs have partnerships with support offices.

> *"Each program partners with one or more local child support enforcement agencies to help address (custody) issues. Representatives from the child support agency provide information to fathers about how to navigate the system, typically during group workshop sessions. The partnerships also pave the way for advocacy by program staff on behalf of some participating fathers."*

---

[24] "Responsible Fatherhood Programs in the Parents and Children Together (PACT) Evaluation" Dion, Zaveri, and Holcomb, AFCC Newsletter, Family Court Review, Vol. 53 No. 2, April 2015 292–303, page 294.

p

The child support office is offering legal services to fathers and is giving preferential treatment to some dads.

Individual legal services are also offered. *"To further assist fathers with paternity, child support, custody and parenting time agreements, some programs offer legal services. These legal services are typically in high demand."* While acknowledging that legal representation is not allowable under the federal grant, fathers still *"can receive free advice from an in-house legal clinic and, for a fee, legal representation. At another program fathers can receive pro bono legal advice through partnership with a local legal aid society."* Legal assistance encourages dads to file custody petitions. *"During a 2-day orientation, legal aid staff spend an afternoon presenting information on the benefits of parenting time agreements and how fathers can petition the court to legally establish such agreements"* (pages 296, 297).

Most fathers join fatherhood programs in order to pursue custody (page 297). These fathers are mature, in their mid-20s and older, and often have children with multiple women. The dads claim mothers create barriers. The dads *"have very difficult backgrounds and face a broad array of socioeconomic challenges with low educational attainment, employment and earnings."* In the month prior to enrollment, 50% lacked jobs, and of those who were employed, 27% earned less than $500. 23% lacked a high school diploma or GED. 58% had a legal child support order. 3/4ths had criminal records. 1/3rd were on parole. The fathers had spent an average of 1.7 years in prison/jail. Half had unstable housing, including living in shelters and halfway homes, residential treatment centers, or temporarily living with a friend or relative.

These demographics would seem to infer that this particular group of dads represents poor candidates for custody, especially given that the child's mother has been the primary caregiver. To counter any existing personality faults, fatherhood programs offer parenting and relationship classes. While custody assistance is in high demand, behavior modification classes are poorly attended with 2/3rds attending only one workshop during the first 4 months of program enrollment. Relationship workshops offered separately had the lowest rates – only 2-15% of enrollees attended half of the relationship group sessions (page 298).

Instead of treating fathers with custody petitions, these dads would benefit from treatment for adverse childhood experiences (http://www.acestudy.org/).

> *"fathers told of childhoods filled with neglect, poverty, and a range of other traumatic experiences. In nearly half of interviews, fathers' stories about their early lives included exposure to substance abuse and domestic violence by parental figures. Most men did not have a positive father role model, describing their own fathers as having been in and out of prison, involved with drugs or alcohol, or simply absent from their lives altogether"* (page 299).

Although the children are currently in the custody of their mother, fatherhood programs assist these problem dads in petitioning for custody, thereby reducing support obligation, an act which will likely inflict the same traumas on their own children.

These dads fight with their children's mother, non-disputed custody arrangements rarely exist.

> *"Fathers face challenges in gaining access to their children. These children's parents are often in acrimonious high-conflict relationships or may be estranged from one another. Because most were never married, they typically do not have a formal child custody or visitation agreement. Maternal gatekeeping was a consistent theme that arose in discussions with low-income nonresidential fathers. While gatekeeping may in some cases be justified, such as*

in cases of domestic abuse, or lack of a suitable venue for fathers and children to visit, it often may simply be a result of unresolved issues between the parents. This was particularly the case when fathers had moved on to another relationship."

Discounting mother's concerns and reasons for limiting fathers custody (for instance his history of negative behavior and inappropriate caregiving), is a reoccurring theme of fatherhood literature. In order to validate that mothers are unnecessarily withholding custody, Mathematica interviews dads who state *"She uses my son and she just creates a situation where, she's very vindictive. I think she's very bitter."* And *"She leaves me out in the dark about literally everything – doctors and all, medical and dental. She doesn't tell me anything… She makes it really hard to be a dad. She strips me from being a father and being the actual really great dad that I want to be and give him the world."* These types of statements are prevalent in custody litigation; abusers frequently "blame" mothers. It is also curious that his behavior landed him in jail, yet her behavior is the problem. It's a sad truth that those requesting government services quickly learn how to manipulate the system - they learn what to say and how to present in order to receive the assistance being offered. These dads know that increasing custody reduces support and they know the program will help them obtain custody as long as it appears he wants to be a "good" father and mom won't let him.

Mathematica does admit reviewers did not speak with the children's mother, the current primary caregiver.

> *"It is important to acknowledge that we do not know the other side of these fathers' stories. Still they suggest that some nonresidential fathers actively seeking to improve their parenting skills may nevertheless struggle to see their children because of unresolved issues with the children's mothers"* (page 300).

It is not considered a factor that even if he is learning to improve his parenting skills, he does not have a history of quality, hands-on parenting, and that, in itself could be the reason mother is concerned about him having unsupervised custody. Most mothers hesitate to give their children to unfit adults, where there could be numerous safety and abuse problems, even if the adult has a genetic tie to the child.

Kids Change Dad's behavior?

Another recurring theme of fatherhood literature is labeled *"children as a catalyst for change."* Fatherhood programs believe that children will be the motivation dads need to change their own behavior – that increasing custody will be the stimulus for dads to turn themselves around whether their old behavior was violence, drug abuse, crime or chronic unemployment. (More information is contained in "Fathering After Violence.")

In conclusion, Mathematica advises programs develop form custody petitions and support modification for fathers to use and to engage low-cost or free community legal services.

Partnerships

"Forging Effective Responsible Fatherhood Partnerships: A Research to Practice Brief"[25] is a fatherhood.gov hand-out written by the SFER team. This brief is important because it confirms that custody and support is a chief component of fatherhood programs. Mathematica staff have a comprehensive understanding of fatherhood programming. In reviewing SFERs, they identified that programs operate "Partnerships." This brief explains and promotes the use of partnerships.

---

[25] "Forging Effective Responsible Fatherhood Partnerships: A Research to Practice Brief"

SFERs identifies three types of partnerships:

a. <u>Contractual</u> – partner is contracted service i.e. counselor.
b. <u>Supplemental</u> – have an established agreement to recruit, provide services, prioritize fathers; i.e. career/job centers (ancillary services to one lead organization).
c. <u>Integrated</u> – partners provide active integral role to provide core program services – parenting education, employment assistance (several organizations).

SFERs identifies three partnerships –

a. <u>Courts and Support Offices (CSE or Domestic Relations)</u> – Support offices are good partners because they can be used for recruitment and offer incentives like a reduction of arrears (support owed), expedited or suspended orders. Another suggestion is to downplay support office involvement by locating staff within the fatherhood program. Family Courts issue binding legal orders and can make fatherhood mandatory for men with debt, or they will go to jail, thus increasing fatherhood program participation. Courts can mandate mediation and other services to increase custody.

b. <u>Employment agencies</u> – The majority of programs only offer soft services – resumes and work behavior. Fathers are referred to already existing centers such as welfare-to-work agencies and state-run unemployment referral centers. A few programs offer career counseling or employment supports such as transportation assistance or money for work supplies such as uniforms and tools. Criminal records, and low education and skills are cited as a barrier to employment.

c. <u>Prisons</u> – Prisons are often a first contact for dads owing support. Dads receive fatherhood programming such as

Inside/Out Dad and 24/7 Dad, and assistance with support modification while incarcerated.

Partnerships offers advice. To get the partnership to work, staff must support the goal, be "on board." For instance: some support staff do not want to address access/visitation when discussing support orders since most support staff say traditionally support and custody are separate. *Strategic Planning Guide* tells states it is ok to tell support staff to inform fathers that obtaining custody will reduce support.

Partnerships tell programs to use a lead agency. The lead agency does not provide services but oversees and coordinates contracted services. It seems possible that the lead agency could be state AV coordinators, or organizations such as the John S. Martinez Fatherhood Initiative of Connecticut.

Partnerships tell programs to use case managers to facilitate services, and to offer fathers "in house" services, for instance: have support staff and attorney's work from the program's location rather than require fathers to visit various locations.

Partnerships stresses the importance of communication and data sharing. For instance, Texas workforce commission sent web-based reports to support court & OAG.

Partnership states fatherhood and ancillary staff must be given appropriate training and time to perform services. For instance, support staff should be trained to expedite prisoners' support orders modification

Recruitment and Retention

Where do programs find dads?

---

[26] "*Recruiting and Retaining Men in Responsible Fatherhood Programs*: A Research to Practice Brief" written by Sarah Avellar

Programs: A Research to Practice Brief[26] addresses fatherhood program recruitment. *Recruit & Retain* suggests recruiting fathers at places they "hang out" such as basketball courts, barber shops and health clinics. *Recruit & Retain* does not make it clear if brochures are left, or if staff appear in person at health clinics and barbershops and solicit men to attend programs. One program tried to recruit dads at the child's doctor visits but they found that dads did not go to the child's doctor visits. This method of recruitment is curious because fatherhood programs are structured to increase dad's custody. A chief parental responsibility is maintaining the physical health of a child. A parent who attends doctor visits would be the better parent and custody is often decided on who currently performs routine child care and parenting functions. *Recruit & Retain* substantiates that the dads they target are not currently high quality, involved caretakers.

Recruit & Retain iterates that passive recruitment does not work well (father contacts the program). One type of passive recruitment assessed is mass mailings to dads with active support orders. A sample recruitment mass mailer was obtained by Doreen Ludwig. The 2-page letter is addressed to a mother who is currently receiving support payments as she is the primary caretaker of several children. Dad owns his business in Massachusetts and, according to mom, is in the top 5% of income earners, with earnings over $400,000 per year. Mom believes she received the solicitation in error. It would appear questionable for a State to proposition high-income dads to reduce their support payments. In an email attaching the recruitment letter, mom wrote

> *"Here is a copy of the letter I got from the Massachusetts Department of Revenue, regarding my ex-husband's child support. I believe that they sent it to me by accident. I have never received any communication from them, certainly not asking if I was having trouble paying my bills or if I had a change in circumstances that would need a*

modification. I would love to know what they would say if I were a man and I called."

Other methods of passive recruitment are billboard and radio ads. Parents with highly litigious cases in Connecticut observed a billboard featuring a WWA wrestler advertising the John S. Martinez Fatherhood Initiative of Connecticut. "Take Time To Be A Dad" is the promotional slogan featured in ads and pamphlets.

A mother who survived a contested custody ordeal informed Doreen Ludwig of a radio ad depicting a father reading a plumbing manual to his child.

> *"Thought you might be interested in knowing that the government is using yet another avenue to entice custody onto unfit fathers. I heard a commercial on a local radio station while driving in my car today. This is how it went. You hear a man reading from a book about plumbing. He goes on for several seconds until he is interrupted by the voice of a small child, it sounds like a girl. She refers to the man as her dad, and suggests to him that he might want to get some real children's books for them to read. The man apologizes and asks if she wants him to stop reading. The girl says no, she is interested in how the story about plumbing ends. Then an announcer provides some phone numbers and makes a reference to fatherhood.gov. I am presuming that the purpose of the commercial is to encourage fathers to seek custody of children."*

> *"The commercial is indicating that the father is oblivious to his child's developmental needs. Is he just wrapped up in his own interests about his work, plumbing, that he does not know that the needs of a child are different than his? The child has to point it out. Is the ad implying that dad is uneducated and unintelligent? But despite his unfitness, the child is supposed to accept him the way he is and learn to like what he likes. The father is unfit, but he's not going*

to change. This makes me so mad because I could see a mother losing custody over an accusation that she did not contribute to the child's education by having reading material for the child."

"I know that some people would say that the message of the commercial is that the father is at least trying to read to the child and that is the most important thing. However, I think that message is drowned out by the overall message that fathers are held to a low standard and deserve to be praised even when they make mistakes. The children are supposed to accept the unfit fathers as they are and not ask for better."

The fatherhood agenda is still going strong. The public is being brainwashed."

Recruit & Retain advises programs to have broad eligibility requirements in order to recruit more men - having age and income limits resulted in low recruitment. SFER found young fathers were hard to recruit. Under SFERs "income" category contained in each program demographics, we find many community programs service non-poverty level men. These two facts contradict the propaganda that the programs serve young, minority, low-income dads.

For active recruitment strategies, prisons and courts are the most productive referral source. *Recruit & Retain* advises fatherhood program staff be stationed in support offices and attend support hearings (pg. 2 & 4). One program avoided advertising because of its relationship with the support office – a better method of recruitment.

Recruit & Retain advises programs to offer services that improve father's circumstances. *"When programs focused on increasing support payments fathers felt no direct benefit since money went to mother"* (page 7). To retain dads, *Recruit& Retain* recommends reducing fatherhood programming from 6 sessions to 2. As noted above, fathers do not attend the healthy relationship and parenting classes, in fact, these classes are a barrier to participation.

SFER found that fathers did not participate in programs after their release from prison.

Mandatory programs linked to court and support offices had higher retention.

Fatherhood.gov and AFCC

Doreen Ludwig of Mothers Against Court Custody Abuse (www.MACCAbuse.org) and Helen Lynn of Protect Our Kids, visited the conference entitled "Advance Issues in Child Custody: Evaluation, Litigation and Settlement," held jointly by American Academy of Matrimonial Lawyers (AAML) and Association of Family and Conciliation Courts (AFCC), billed as "two premier family law organizations." Notable seminars include: "Alienation and High Conflict" and "Shared Legal Custody: Should There Be A Presumption?"

Two (2) "Take Time to Be a Dad" pamphlets were retrieved from the National Responsible Fatherhood Clearinghouse (NRFC), (known by its web domain name "fatherhood.gov"), staffed table. Pamphlet language confirms fatherhood.gov ignores the prevalence of deep-seated paternal abuse.

> **#1) *"Unbreakable Bond – The Strength of a Father's Love"***
>
> *"Research has shown that a father's love is just as important as – or sometimes even more important than – a mother's love."*

"Studies have demonstrated that young people whose fathers are actively involved in their lives have greater self-confidence, perform better in school, and are better able to avoid risky behaviors."

#2) **"Healthy Relationships – Letting Go of the Past"**

"Many of us carry into our adult relationships the dysfunctional behaviors we witnessed and learned as children. If your parents separated or divorced, or if one parent abandoned the family, you could have adopted the same behavior patterns that prompted these events."

"If your relationships in the past were stormy or troubled, you can start now to undo attitudes and behaviors that might have contributed to an unsatisfying personal life. By understanding how early circumstances have had an impact on your life, you can begin to overcome negative habits and thinking that can affect your relationships now and in the future."

This brochure refers readers to TwoofUS.org, a website funded by government marriage promotion and private foundations advocating for marriage.

Fatherhood.gov pamphlet propaganda belittles the harm caused when children are forced to exist with severe abuse.

Are Dads All Children Need?

Contrary to propaganda, the Centers for Disease Control (CDC) conducted the ACE study (Adverse Childhood Experiences) which confirmed that poor outcomes can be attributed to abuse and traumatic experiences – child maltreatment - <u>not</u> to lack of a male authority figure within the home. The CDC defines maltreatment as physical abuse, sexual abuse, psychological abuse and neglect.

To assure all children reach their full potential, the CDC asserts children must be given safe, stable and [appropriate] nurturing relationships and environments. The CDC has written "Essentials for Childhood Framework" – download at https://www.cdc.gov/violenceprevention/childmaltreatment/essentials.html

Fatherhood programs do not incorporate this important CDC knowledge. Children are severely harmed and traumatized by a family court system that routinely takes away their stable, lifetime, appropriately nurturing mother and gives custody to an unsafe father merely to prop-up the male regime. Children - male and female - are harmed when society diverts enormous funds to propping up the male regime.

CHAPTER SIX

Contested Custody v. Dispute Resolution

Family court is a system. Special interests built the structure. Co-parenting is the premise. Resolution of dispute is asserted to be the goal of mediation. Quality parenting can be learned. Kindness and cooperation can be dictated from above.

Abuse is multi-faceted and deep-seated. Abuse is an outcome of unequal power. Abuse is a distorted application of authority. Abuse is **not** an argument. Should targets be sheltered by the system?

In truth, forced shared parenting is a system set-up to generate profits. Court appointees pretend abuse is a disagreement that they can correct. In truth, shared parenting custody orders are a technique employed by abusers to win full control.

This book is not about the 5-10% of couples who mutually decide a joint arrangement will work for their family – who are seriously committed to making the best of divorce - who can mutually self-determine without the aid of litigators and court appointees. This book is about weaponized litigation.

Abusive Dads contest custody

Parents of minor children who live apart and can't agree must let court to decide custody. There are two designations: legal and physical. Legal custody implies decision-making authority: medical, educational, activities, etc. Physical custody signifies the hours a parent possesses the child. Historically, a primary caregiving mother was given primary physical and legal custody. Dads who did not parent before divorce did not request and receive primary parenting rights upon divorce. Those men were given physical custody every other weekend and a few hours during the week. The arrangement created a primary home and structure for the child – constant and dependable routines and surroundings, a familiar bed, stability. Continuity of care took precedence over personal longing.

Mothers who are abused have typically been the primary care giver. His attitude is indifferent and unwilling. He feels housework and childcare are lowly women's work. He may enforce rules – but he rarely undertakes chores himself.

Typically, at the onset of litigation, mothers have primary physical and legal custody. Once litigation begins and court service providers become involved, custody shifts. Men pursue financial and power advantages of winning. In the worst cases, Dad gains sole custody - frequently blind-siding mother and child in a one-day traumatic court maneuver.

Is shared parenting the answer?

Father's rights and fatherhood movements advanced the notion dads parenting was not only equal, but superior to moms, even when previously non-existent. Father's rights advocates wrote books and internet sites detailing custody litigation tactics, formed and joined organizations to promote men and lobby congress for funding. Pretending to be for "shared parenting" and "children's rights," men masked their agenda of oppression of women and children doled out in judicial custody determinations.

The avalanche of lobbying, promotion and funding, created a culture where co-parenting is preferential. Each parent gets equal amounts of time. The children move between two homes. The child's environment is changed every other week, every day, or every 3-4 days.

Could there be a different reality to the idyllic shared parenting family?

> "I didn't need an overnight bag; my parents had done what they could to avoid a situation where I'd be packing and unpacking twice a week, and I had two rooms outfitted with essentials and beyond — two pairs of pink-framed glasses, two closets full of clothing, two favorite stuffed animals." (Bergstein NY Times blogpost)

In theory, custody orders that give equal amounts of time to both genders appear innocuous. But are they? Do judges consider the reason for the relationship dissolution? Was the divorce action prompted by a history of mistreatment? Physical attacks? Permeation of an atmosphere of male superiority and oppression? Preferential or situational pedophilia?

Abusive males contest custody. Litigation is a tactic of punishment and control. Abusers fight to "win" – asking for half-time physical possession often not giving up until they gain complete legal and physical ownership. Parents who share children have continuous interaction. They must be able to work in conjunction to meet the child's needs. Do trumpian abusers have the capacity to work with anyone? Working together for a child means your self-interest is secondary, sometimes third. What about men who, when they feel offended, hit back ten times harder? Who believe everyone else exists to feed their narcissistic needs? Is shared parenting a vehicle ridden by abusers to complete control?

The Dilemma

Should an abused child be forced to spend half of their growing years with a dangerous parent? A negligent one? A parent who insists the child conforms to illogical demands? A parent who believes others exist to pacify and please them? Who feels superior to women and children? Who has never participated in caregiving? Who is willing to hand over care to a paid employee, parent or new relationship? Who pouts when the child studies?

Should a mother who performed all caregiving duties be ordered not only to "share" but to adhere to a strict regimen, reporting every action back to their abuser?

The benefits of shared parenting to abusers are large. He gains continued access to his victims. He maintains control and dominance even after divorce. He wins financially as any support owed is largely reduced. When awarded primary custody, he can collect support from mom. He can claim a child tax exemption. He can align himself with court employees and appointees to force mother and child to his will and punish any protestation.

What happens when a system refuses to acknowledge that shared parenting is not a viable option for families of abuse?

Shared parenting is renamed "Parallel Parenting"

The industry knows that abusers are irredeemable – that their behavior and actions do not change – so the court renames abuse "high conflict" and the court appoints an overseer – to settle disputes in private, in an appointee's office, off the judicial record. Parallel Parenting is an alternative mode proposed to subject families to all levels of daily life management by government-enabled intruders.

The Arizona arm of the trade group AFCC developed *"The Summit Project"* in 2011.[27] Court dignitaries and trade group members market protocols for judicial orders for parents who don't get along but are required to share custody. The inability to work

---

[27] "The Summit Project" http://www.afccnet.org/Resource-Center/Resources-for-Professionals

effectively together is not deemed a barrier. Co-parenting is renamed "parallel parenting." Each adult parents the child during the timeframe they house the child. These adults do not work together – they work in the same direction under an order of the court with oversight for adherence being assigned to a fee-driven third party. The judge orders a means of communication – a notebook, a calendar, a reporting form or internet program. Parents who fail to follow instructions are sanctioned – jail, money fines, loss of custody and supervised visits.

Types of court-ordered communication include:

- Child News Report – each parent must report details of their interactions with their child. For infants and toddlers - naps, feeding, bedtime routines, disciplinary actions, soothing techniques, potty training, moods, medical and developmental news and concerns. For school-age kids – bed, bath and meal routines, behavior and discipline, homework and school activities, outside school activities, and peer relationships.

    Judges can order parents to use a notebook, email, or internet program such as those marketed by AFCC conference attendees (familywizard.com, sharekids.com, jointparent.com and parentingtime.net). The order contains a deadline for when each parent must report back to the other parent, such as by Sunday 10:00p.m.

- The 12-month calendar – One parent gets to fill-in a calendar a year [month, week] in advance choosing which days they will physically house the child, and noting any events or scheduled activities. In theory, the other parent is permitted to comment and suggest changes. Each parent must submit their agreement to adhere to the calendar in writing to the court.

- ❖ <u>Supplemental judicial orders</u> may decree a parent share information so that the other parent may decide and approve education, medical including emergency, treatment, and get approval from the other parent to arrange activities that occur during that parents time, such as participation in team sports, dance or karate lessons.

Ostensibly, these parallel parenting orders solve the problem of relationship dysfunction. In actually, the encroachment into every aspect of the other parents' family life leaves ample opportunity for an exploiter to taint and distort for the goal of switching custody to the manipulator. Another beauty of the parallel parenting order is the ability of the abuser to indoctrinate the child through a slow process of undermining the other parent. Every exchange, every moment with the child is an opportunity for an abuser to insidiously undermine the other parent.

Parallel parenting encourages misuse

Because family court has been structured to be a male supremacist organization, with males being given more weight (a legal term denoting legitimacy), parallel parenting orders are skewed in his favor. He is permitted to pick the schedule – she is required to agree. He is given authority to veto continuous activities that interfere with his "parenting time." He is given primary legal custody which means he is solely permitted to determine medical treatment, educational goals and social activities. Mothers are required to concede or face punishment. Mothers that argue for the safety, health and interests of their child deserve the most severe of sanctions – a switch of custody to dad and loss of joint physical custody.

In a New York Times blog post written by Rachelle Bergstein,[28]

---

[28] Rachelle Bergstein, AFCC Featured Family Law News
http://well.blogs.nytimes.com/2016/07/08/the-secret-superpower-of-a-sharedcustodykid/?rref=collection/timestopic/Families%20and%20Family%20Li

touted in an AFCC newsletter as being proof that co-parenting is best for a child, we find subtle facets of father's underlying abusive nature, its effect on his child, and the courts willingness to let dad dictate the schedule.

> "at the start of every month, my father listed the nights I would spend with him and then presented my mother with a copy. His diligence was a safeguard against situations just like this one, when he rang the doorbell to an empty house and then let the frustration and resentment wash over him."

Feeling frustrated and resentful when another parent is late for an exchange is indicative of a man who cannot handle life events that do not operate in his favor. Making fun of traits like tardiness and manners, sulking when not being given attention, chaos and instability, while not highly abusive, contribute to a child's mental confusion and anxiety.

> "...as I tipped into my teenage years, switching back and forth became more difficult. There were, of course, small aggravations, like when I accidentally left something I wanted at the other house. Yet that didn't account for the new anxiety I felt at those twice-weekly hand-offs."

> "...my mom went back to school and our house was quiet, our conversations intellectual. My dad had two more little girls, and every time I stepped through the front door, it felt like I'd joined the circus. Mom stressed the importance of academic achievement; Dad pouted when, in our limited time together, I shut my door to do my homework. My mother thought manners were a sign of good breeding, and she frequently appended a "please" to the end of my requests. When I asked my father for "a glass of orange

---

fe&action=click&contentCollection=timestopics®ion=stream&module=stream_unit&version=latest&contentPlacement=1&pgtype=collection&_r=1

juice, please," he ribbed me for behaving like a guest in my own kitchen."

It may have been her mother's behavior that kept Rachel's anxiety from becoming a full melt-down – mom's intellectualism, mom's ignoring of dad's belittling and bullying, mom's resilience. A new wife and children gave Dad a new focus for his immaturity and attention demands. Some fathers, noting their daughter's dismay, would have backed off from demanding sleep-overs on school nights - instead settling for daytime visits without weekday stay-overs. Father's rights feel their needs precede alleviating a child's discomfort.

Whilst minimizing her dad's contrary traits, Rachel concludes the youthful instability built a resilient character. Not all children of parallel parenting families are so lucky. Many live with severely threatening and dangerous dads. Incest is not automatically a crime. Physical assaults are minimized and encouraged by court appointees who tell dad to assert his authority. Many local police and child protection services will not investigate abuse when there is an active court custody order. These children live with continuous devaluation of self. They live with oppression. Sometimes the fit parent is demoralized and destroyed by the custody battle. Financial impoverishment, fear of retaliation, continued harassment, inability to improve their circumstances, leaves a child fluctuating between a dominating parent and a disheartened one.

In *Motherless America* I tell the story of a New Jersey family ordered to co-parenting services of Dr. Barry Bricklin, a promoter of Richard Gardner's Parental Alienation Syndrome. Dad hired Bricklin and his cohort Gail Elliot to oversee his custody case. In many regards, the Judge made Bricklin head of this family. With Bricklin, Dad dictated the weekly schedule. Mom, a retail manager, never knew which days she would have to leave work and pick up her daughters and when she would have to take them to dad's house. When the children failed to obey, Bricklin told Dad to assert his authority by hitting and punishing. When the children still resisted Dad's sexual advances and physical harm, they were institutionalized at The Rachel Foundation in Texas. Mom spent all her and her parent's financial resources attempting to speak for her two children in family court. It was only when the girls aged-out that Dad lost interest. Ten years later, Dad has no interest in the children he fought so diligently to control during their youth.

Who, What, When and How of Shared Parenting

A second industry generated booklet informs us of the mindset of court orders. AFCC members in Massachusetts wrote *"Planning for Shared Parenting: A Guide for Parents Living Apart."*[29] The shared parenting guide contains a disclaimer that it is not appropriate in domestic violence situations. Undisclosed is the fact that the majority of contested custody cases involve high levels of psychological, and financial abuse and are more likely to involve and devolve into sexual abuse of the child. The shared parenting guide looks at physical custody parameters for each age group. For infants and toddlers, the guide recommends dads have frequent contact – every day and no less than two days apart. The shared parenting guide states *"even if the parent has never participated in caregiving they should be given ample opportunity to master feeding, playing, bathing, soothing, putting infant to sleep (nap or night)."* Under this schism a full-time mother will be ordered to hand-over the child or children to dad almost daily so that he may build a bond which didn't exist until the onset of litigation. The frequent contact shared parenting order lets abusers maintain psychological domination. In that vein, the shared parenting guide insists parents use a communication log. As the child ages, parents are coached to

---

[29] Planning for Shared Parenting: A Guide for Parents Living Apart written by Massachusetts AFCC –http://www.mass.gov/courts/docs/courts-and-judges/courts/probate-and-family-court/afccsharedparenting.pdf

allow the child greater independence for self-activities and friends. (Abusers can be highly dependent and isolating.) The shared parenting guide lists good and bad examples of parent interaction. Once again, an AFCC-generated document alludes to miraculously solve the myriad of ways abuse is expressed.

Post-Judgment Custody Switch

Abused mothers are coached by lawyers and coerced by court affiliates to agree to shared parenting orders. Many agree to lucrative, father-led deals, with fee-driven third parties being appointed to mediate disputes. Dad, who never parented, receives half-time overnights. Mom, who performs all child care activity, receives secondary status. Every other day the children must live .in a different home. The court enters a final judgment in the divorce matter. Statistically, there is an appearance of equality, or of mothers receiving higher amounts of primary custody. However, coparenting situations frequently have two litigation results –

(1) Dad maltreats the children during his time; mom raises the issue of abuse and asks the court for a reduction of dad's access; mom is psychologically labeled and ignored; dad is awarded sole custody.
(2) Ongoing frequent interaction gives dads ample fodder to make far-fetched allegations of mom's unfitness; without evidence, dad is awarded sole custody and control.

Promoting Tactics

Fathers' rights websites give dads advice ranging from the overtly angry to mild mannered counsel couched in subtleties. Simple google searches of "father's rights" and "custody for dads" supply volumes. Text extracted from two sites show the obfuscation "sell."

Farzad law firm in California uses articles to promote its services. "How to get custody as a father" led me to a post with topics of "Divorcing a high conflict personality versus a narcissist; sociopath; borderline or bipolar; addict; and gatekeeper."[30] This article explains the different parameters that will be used to pathologize the other parent. (Underlines contain analogous articles.) While family court merely terms contested custody "high conflict," mental health practitioners are in the habit of submitting reports with outlandish accounts of severe pathology, predominately against mothers who are primary caregivers.

Farzad's website shows us the insidious nature behind the generalized high conflict label. While the system calls all protracted litigation "high conflict," lawyers and mental health workers advertise a range of illnesses designed to cover-up and excuse abuse of the child.

Under *"Divorcing a high conflict personality versus a gatekeeper"* Farzad states gatekeepers are *"more than overprotective parents – we consider them a unique personality type."*

> *"A gatekeeper is protective of the child to an unreasonable degree. We call them restrictive gatekeepers...they are unreasonable, and take their actions to the level of emotional abuse of the children. They can engage in parental alienation."*

> *"Gatekeepers are obsessive and, on the extreme end, delusional....they conjure up scenarios in their head of how dangerous the other parent may be to the children. The more obsessive and delusional – the more restrictive."*

> *"Some are fanatical in their belief system. They are 'true believers' in their own nonsense which is unsupported by*

[30] http://farzadlaw.com/divorce-in-california/how-to-get-custody-as-a-father/

> *any reasonable evidence or is founded on exaggerated revisionist history...are histrionic...often make false allegations of abuse."*
>
> *"Restricted gatekeepers play the victim role. They can be passive, emotional and sometimes quite convincing...they come across as protective and loving parents who just want the best for their children."*

Farzad recommends *"proper litigation," "strategic planning" "the right attorney for the job" "a skilled trial lawyer."*

> *"Certain divorce attorneys are not built for litigation....when you are hiring someone to deal with a high conflict personality in your spouse you need more than a good negotiator. You need a good litigator. Attorneys who are skilled litigators do not spend an unreasonable amount of time trying to resolve issues."*

Farzad informs potential clients *"a skilled litigator will not spend time resolving issues amicably. Your attorney must have the courage to take the case to the courtroom or you are doomed."*

> *"Because high conflict personalities rarely do the right thing easily. The great majority of the time, you have to give a high conflict personality something serious to lose to get them to cooperate and negotiate in good faith."*

Farzad recommends a litigation plan which includes requesting judicial orders for custody and support; requesting your attorney fees should be paid for by your spouse (this requires charges that she is the cause of litigation); and, appointment of experts such as custody evaluators.

> *"Proactive litigation strategy disarms the high conflict personality because it takes control away."*

These excerpts are a brief example of nefarious counsel. Courts are vowing to cure high conflict. All the while attorneys are strategizing to win.

A second attorney posts a line of attack on fathersrights.org website. Using a checklist, men are advised to *"clean out bank accounts" "cancel credit cards" "hire an attorney who has a reputation as a fighter" "do not move out of the home unless ordered by the court" "take video and pictures of you with the children" "become involved in your child's school activities" "perform all childcare functions"* and *"tape all conversations with your spouse."* Men are warned *"DO NOT ALLOW NEW GIRLFRIENDS TO INTERMEDDLE UNTIL LITIGATION IS DONE"* and *"Make NO threats of violence. EVER."*[31]

These are examples of just two forces behind family court. Are they outside the radar? Outliers or common? Looking at these websites and other resources marketed to dads, confirms that abusers are encouraged and aided to concoct manipulative litigation tactics. They are coached to keep obvious signs of harm hidden during litigation.

Do abused women and their children have a comparative network working to protect them? Sadly, the answer is "NO." In keeping with the for-profit scheme that runs family court, local domestic violence (DV) staff and national DV groups that claim to advocate for women, concurrently built their own network of family court specialists.

Counteraction or Complicity?

The Office of Violence Against Women (OVW) funds a few groups

[31] http://www.fathersrights.org/index-old.html

that portray themselves as being able to train family court operatives in the complex nature of abuse. With money earmarked to help victims, OVW grantees work with insiders to write primers for practitioners to use to distinguish true abuse from the gatekeepers, alienators, sociopaths, and others described on Farzod's site. The resulting "how-to-define-abuse" primers are available on AFCC's website.

The Battered Women's Justice Project (BWJP)[32] is a premier domestic violence grant awardee working with AFCC to educate industry insiders in the ways of abusive males. Wingspread Conference was an initial attempt to have three groups - AFCC, BWJP, NCJFCJ - work together. Wingspread concluded *"All high conflict cases should have a co-parenting coordinator assigned to manage day-to-day decision-making and ongoing education."*[33]

Loretta Frederick, J.D. received her legal degree from Mitchell Hamline School of Law. She has a long history of working within the criminal area of the domestic violence community. Frederick is a Senior Legal Policy advisor for BWJP. Claiming to be working to improve outcomes in custody where there is domestic violence, Frederick works with several judicial groups including NCJFCJ and National Judicial Institute on Domestic Violence. In 2007, in conjunction with NCJFCJ and Janet Johnson, Frederick presented an AFCC pre-conference institute on classifying abuse. Frederick participated in Wingspread conference and OCSE's ~~fatherhood roundtable - two~~ AFCC and NCJFCJ protocol

[32] "Report From The Wingspread Conference on Domestic Violence and Family Courts" Ver Steegh, Dalton, page 12.
[33] Judicial Officers Institute: Domestic Violence and Differentiation, AFCC 2007 pre-conference institute
http://www.bwjp.org/our-work/projects/national-child-custody-project.html
http://www.bwjp.org/our-work/projects/safer.html
https://mitchellhamline.edu/dispute-resolution-institute/
https://mitchellhamline.edu/biographies/person/nancy-ver-steegh/

implementation events.

Gabrielle Davis, is a second BWJP legal policy advisor, and member of AFCC. Davis frequently authors articles for AFCC publication including one jointly authored with Ver Steegh on the topic of child support and custody. Davis is an editor of AFCC's newsletter, Family Court Review. Davis works on BWJP's National Custody Demonstration Project promoting the use of DV assessment tools.

Nancy Ver Steegh obtained a masters of social work and law degree. Ver Steegh has deep roots within AFCC, including stints as its president. Ver Steegh reviewed a draft of "High Conflict Parent Education" written by AFCC's Peter Salem, identified as one of five premier documents that outline family court operations. As a professor at Mitchell Hamline School of Law, Ver Steegh advances BWJP DV primers. As a senior fellow at Mitchell's Dispute Resolution Institute, Ver Steegh advances mediation and conflict, or dispute, resolution. Mitchell's Dispute Resolution Institute featured the work of BWJP's National Child Custody Project as an innovative approach to mediation and domestic violence.

Building on the premise that an appointee can cure what ails families - BWJP received an OVW grant to draw-up a template which could be applied by appointees to determine if abuse exists. The result – *Practice Guides for Family Court Decision-making* - is available for download on BWJP's and AFCC's websites.[34] Because BWJP's guide attempts to "solve every problem" it is chaotic, frenetic and confusing – as if the authors "threw everything against the wall in the hopes that something would stick." BWJP's guide is overly detailed yet unspecific. Harm is given no priority – yelling is equated with using children in pornography. Frequency, value and intent are missing elements.

---

[34] http://www.afccnet.org/Portals/0/PublicDocuments/practice-guides-for-family-court-decision-making-ind.pdf

Because abuse is all-inclusive – almost any non-pristine behavior is suspect. BWJP's guide leaves a lot of room for the ill-informed, or ill-motivated, to wrongly assign blame.

Pages 25-27 lists attributes and behaviors to look for. Emotional abuse of a child includes: calling the child names; making the child feel stupid or inadequate; creating a chaotic or unpredictable home life; missing visits; modeling bad behavior; breaking promises; disrupting the child's structure or routine; violating the child's boundaries; and, vacillating between parenting styles.

Physical and sexual abuse and neglect are lumped together in one category and includes: hitting, punching, slapping and pushing the child; promoting truancy; using excessive and/or coercive discipline; exposing the child to drugs; violating the child's physical privacy; and, forcing the child to have sex with others.

Economic abuse includes: depleting bank accounts; destroying other parent's credit; selling other parent's property; and, trading money or support for time with the child.

These are just a small sample of listed behaviors. It would seem that some – sexual abuse - should cause an immediate loss of physical custody while others appear to set an unachievably high standard of perfect parent conduct.

Under a section called "Guiding Principles for Mediation – Knowing and Voluntary Participation" (page 49) BWJP admits that before participating in mediation, a parent would have to give "informed consent" to: *"relinquish their right to offer evidence, examine witnesses and create a record; relinquish their right to have a decision made on the merits (of the case); and, relinquish their right to appeal."* The glaring difference between DV and AFCC lawyers is their willingness to in-word-only divulge the lack of due process protection inherent in the mediation scheme.

On page 53, in a section entitled "Assessing Readiness for Co-parenting" BWJP tells the appointee to identify the "functional" co-parent because *"parenting responsibilities and authority is often relegated or delegated to someone else – extended family, new partners, paid employee or others."* Mothers will attest that dads are frequently given custody only to hand-over caregiving duties to someone else – even to the children themselves. Abusive fathers are especially known to litigate and abdicate.

On pages 55-57 we find BWJP's wish list for how courts can enforce co-parenting when there is a history of abuse. Ironically, the suggestions foretell of years of entrenchment of family court appointees into daily life. Ignoring the patriarchy bias prevalent within family court, BWJP still proposes courts "limit abusive parents rulemaking or decision making authority" using a variety of dictatorial methods, for instance:
- *"grant parallel legal custody with deviations under prescribed circumstances"* (Parallel parenting is not applicable to legal custody- two parents cannot separately make medical and educational decisions. Parallel parenting was developed to institute physical custody – a distinction misunderstood by BWJP.)
- *"appoint a parenting consultant to confer with abusive parent on all major decisions"*
- *"appoint a compliance monitor paid for by the abusive parent."*

In a pilot project to test the effectiveness of an original version, BWJP found court appointees were unwilling to apply it. Abusers use litigation to remain dominant – they will never pay for a third-party to tell them how to conduct themselves. Abusers will pay someone to aid their destruction.

BWJP is fully aware that appointees are loathe to use the BWJP guide due to its time-consuming complexity. Additionally, court appointees are predominantly attached to father's rights and fatherhood ideology. Appointees work to make money, not to spend endless hours on disclosure, validation and deduction. BWJP's guide is open to cherry-picking as the attributes and behaviors enumerated are open to distortion and misinterpretation. Lay BWJP's harmful acts over Farzad's articles on mother-pathologies to uncover the expansive variety of obfuscation currently employed by court appointees.

BWJP's guide is not a court administration document like *Strategic Planning Guide* and *Triage Intake Screen*. No abused mother is assured adherence to this primer. No abused mother is assured the insiders involved in her case will abide by, take note of, or even permit her to submit this information into the record. No judge is required to make judicial orders based on BWJP's guide. Given reality within the courtroom – actual case events – BWJP's guide is merely a fanciful daydream applied in an alternate universe.

What is the significance of BWJP accepting OVW grant money to write protocols for family court industry insiders? Subterfuge? Controlled opposition? An AFCC mask? A way to silence abused mothers entrapped in the litigation nightmare?

The safety conundrum

Fatherhood funding mandates dads are awarded custody. AFCC markets its mediation network to resolve issues of harm. It is well-known that co-parenting is not optimal in situations with high amounts of male control. The greatest form of abuse in family court is mothers will – her resistance to his mistreatment – because male domination is condoned.

Instead of advocating for a change in policy, the domestic violence community has developed its own lingo - "safety." Family court players are well aware of dads' mistreatment. Rather than inform abused mothers and children that family court operates a fatherhood custody mandate out of support administrative units, DV affiliates expound "safety first" in a misguided attempt to improve outcomes for children. Rather than acknowledge the existence of a male supremacist structure, DV tells moms that "safety" will work.

An AFCC published article, written by Ver Steegh and Davis,[35] promotes the assessment of domestic violence of the parent - **not** maltreatment of the children – **not** parenting history and ability - at the onset of support litigation. When a party files for support – litigation begins. Support orders are never issued without litigation - whether or not a party has hired an attorney or are self-represented (pro se). The DV assessment has been developed because fatherhood incorporates custody litigation into support litigation. While tying support to custody is portrayed as being for never-married parents only, most divorcing mothers file for - and initially receive - support payments (until custody is switched to father). A stay-at-home mother has no income and depends on support and alimony until she is able to find employment. A mother entrapped in litigation has little hope of becoming self-sufficient.

The contradictions admitted within this article are most notable. Davis and Ver Steegh acknowledge that abusers use custody litigation to further abuse (pg. 282). They admit that requesting government assistance such as cash assistance, housing subsidies or food stamps, forces abused women to file for support payments and thereby custody litigation.

Davis and Ver Steegh admit mediation services run out of the support office have no due process protection.

---

[35] "Calculating Safety: Reckoning Domestic Violence in the Context of Child Support Parenting Time Initiatives" Ver Steegh, Davis, Family Court Review, Vol. 53 No. 2, April 2015, 279-291.

"Proceeding to court, instead of mediating, should be an easily available option for never-married parents. Traditional courts are not a panacea for parents with a history of domestic abuse, but for some they offer much needed protection in the form of due process guarantees, protective orders, enforcement mechanisms, and clear focus on the best interests of children (page 286)."

"....parents should have the opportunity and support necessary to make voluntary and informed choices about participation in dispute resolution and traditional court processes. Not only are substantive decisions about [custody] complex and challenging where domestic violence is involved, but so too are procedural decisions about what processes to use to determine custody (page 285)."

Are Davis and Ver Steegh unaware that jurisdictions operate quasi-judicial hearings where lawyers given judicial powers determine support and custody? That these "conciliation" hearings operate in lieu of mediation? That *Triage Intake Screen* insists all high conflict parents be assigned a court mediation service? Are Davis and Ver Steegh advocating for an opt-out?
.

Look Before You Leap – Triage Intake Screen[36]

In fact, Frederick, Davis and Ver Steegh question the appropriateness of *Triage Intake Screen* in a jointly written article

---

[36] Look Before You Leap: Court Systems Triage of Family Law Cases Involving Intimate Partner Violence" Ver Steegh, Frederick, Davis, 2012
http://open.mitchellhamline.edu/facsch/239

which asks *"What dispute resolution processes are appropriate in cases where there is domestic violence?"* The authors expound: Triage [prioritizing worst cases] merely assigns a service, court employees and appointees misidentify the problem, use personal biases, nor comprehend what can be done about it (page 969). The article is an attempt to compel courts to apply BWJP's guide; to assess the nature and context of physical assault. (See assessment of Triage Intake Screen, Chapter "Modus Operandi.")

Ironically, this article is best at pointing out what is currently wrong with the system – why and how abusers use the system to gain advantage. The authors seem to conclude that woman should be informed before agreeing to participate in court ordered services. Abused mothers should give consent before cooperating in mediation services as ignorance of abuse may result in a poor conclusion. The authors even acknowledge that disclosure of abuse often results in an erroneous outcome (psychological labeling of mother; reunification therapy for child). The number one reason abused mothers are demolished in family court is due to the fact that once they enter a court appointees office they give away their right to due process. BWJP confirms this event, yet attempts to solve it - not through legislative action or executive oversight- but by imploring AFCC members to play nice.

CHAPTER SEVEN

SPECIAL INTERESTS V. TRUTH & JUSTICE

Domestic Violence is a special interest. Evan Stark, author of *"Coercive Control: How Men Entrap Women in Personal Lives"*,[37] explains DVs evolution into "an economy of victimization." Dependence on government funding replaced commitment to women's freedom. Addiction to funding parameters requires stagnation. The Office of Violence Against Women works for Welfare Reform – patriarchy goals of fatherhood and marriage promotion – which leaves out protection from abuse for women with children. Abuse is a range of behaviors especially suited to litigious, diabolical men. Abuse cannot always be cured. Safety is a narrow measure. Mothers are commonly labeled unsafe in a litigation tactic, when they leave and attempt to stop father's harm.

Family Court Special Interest

While DV staff do not act on behalf of abused mothers in custody or support court, they sit on judicial commissions that write protocols for family court administration. HHS, which oversees family court, also operates Fatherhood and Marriage Promotion Programs. Access/Visitation is a fatherhood grant operated under the Office of Child Support Enforcement (OCSE). OCSE's *Strategic Planning Guide* tells states to set-up commissions or task forces to implement the fatherhood program. Father's rights, trade

---

[37] "Coercive Control: How Men Entrap Women in Personal Life" Stark, Evan, 2007, Oxford University Press, Part I: The Domestic Violence Revolution: Promise and Disappointment

association members and domestic violence staff collaborate to design internal family court protocols that are extremely harmful to mothers trying to stop father's abuse. *Strategic Planning Guide* has one objective: to use the authority of family court to increase custody for dads via support office staff, third-party court appointees, and judicial orders.

Support office employees are told to inform fathers of their right to custody and to assist those men in filing legal actions. If a mother fails to agree to increase father's custody, the couple is sent to a court "service" which could be evaluation or mediation.

Pennsylvania's OCSE *Strategic Planning Guide* is called *"Changing the Culture of Custody in Pennsylvania."* The commission included members of Pennsylvania Coalition Against Domestic Violence (PCADV), as well as several trade association members, and judges later disgraced in racism and sexism scandals. Father's rights groups were heavily involved in the passage of partnering legislation.

Changing the Culture of Custody in Pennsylvania merely advances the appointment of for-profit businesspersons to make custody determinations. In order to address the problem of known violent offenders receiving custody, PCADV concurred that an intake screen developed by AFCC was a sufficient mechanism for protection.

Triage Intake Screen

For family court cases that have abuse issues *Changing the Culture of Custody* implements AFCC's *Triage Intake Screen*. PCADV staff that sat on the commission agree that *Triage Intake Screen* represents "The Gold Standard" for processing cases with a history of abuse. *Triage Intake Screen* Is a measure devised by members of AFCC originally for the state of Connecticut. Rather than view abuse as a multi-faceted psychological behavior with ramifications that result in severe physical, mental, sexual, and financial harm to partners and offspring, abuse is minimized and called "conflict." The screen measures parents' conflict – how much they agree and communicate. Mothers who refuse to let father dominate are ruled obstructive, hostile and uncooperative. Men who have been criminally prosecuted for domestic violence are rated as having low communication skills. After one year of no incident, violent men are deemed no longer dangerous.

In designing this DV screen, AFCC relied heavily on AFCC publications, member articles, books, unpublished reports, information gathered from AFCC members, and the domestic violence writings of Janet Johnston. By assessing level of conflict, the authors surmise court employees called "family relations counselors or specialists" can figure out what court services are appropriate to order. The higher the disagreement, the quicker the couple will be sent to third-party decision-makers. Rather than conduct a due process hearing or trial, the court automatically orders an evaluator or lawyer for the children. The appointee is not required to assess parental history or fitness. The appointee is permitted to determine if abuse is currently occurring. Standards and conventions are left to their own discretion – often methods and conclusions have been developed by the father's rights movement and marketed through AFCC conferences. The appointee's conclusions are henceforth treated as "evidence." The appointee is enabled to recommend (and even write) custody orders. All of this occurs outside of a due process environment: off-the-record, without adherence to rules of evidence or law.

Triage Intake Screen is a premier document for understanding the thorough distortion of legal process within family court. It is an example of the "collaboration" between fatherhood programs, father's rights groups, domestic violence staff, family court profiteers and trade association members.

In the past, mental health trained appointees were used in an information-gathering capacity by judges assumed to be "too busy" to conduct in depth judicial hearings and trials over contested custody litigation. However, courts have turned away from the "cause" of divorce breakup and *"custody evaluations that emphasized the identification of parenting abilities and assessment of primary parent-child relationships" (page 4)*. This switch permits courts and appointees to discount abuse and other behaviors that negatively influence parenting, and conversely, behaviors that positively influence parenting.

The American Psychological Association created guidelines for custody evaluations which include verifying facts (evidence) by way of collateral witnesses and assessment of parenting ability and the parent/child "fit." Adherence to these accepted guidelines is deemed ethical. Stepping outside of the industry standard is unethical. Because abusers would be found unfit, the industry created *Triage Intake Screen* to base parenting ability solely on whether parents can cooperate and communicate. Contested custody litigation is a dispute to be resolved by family court for-profit affiliates.

> *"This proliferation of dispute resolution processes has resulted in an exciting range of opportunities for service providers and users alike. What has not developed alongside these services is a clear set of criteria to help determine the optimal fit between clients and the services that best meet their needs" (page 6).*

Contested custody is an opportunity for service providers to profit from the problems of others; contention and abuse generate huge profits. *"Research indicates that a majority of couples succeed in moving beyond the anger, conflict and depression associated with divorce within two to three years following separation, as many as 1/3rd of divorcing couples report significant conflict over children many years later" (page 6).*

Because Triage Intake Screen extrapolates Johnston's ideas, serious abusive conduct is discounted. Families are labeled "failed divorces."

> "high conflict parents are identified by high rates of litigation, high degrees of anger and distrust, incidents of verbal abuse, intermittent physical aggression, and ongoing difficulty communicating about and cooperating over the care of their children. These children bear an acutely heightened risk of repeating the cycle of conflicted and abusive relationships as they grow up and try to form families of their own."

Rather than protect those who are the subject of maltreatment, *Triage Intake Screen* is designed to force them into everlasting relationships of litigation and third-party decision-making, often under highly unequitable financial conditions – whereby the abuser maintains his economic advantage. Do DV staff honor victims when they countenance?

Roundtable – Who's on Top

The Office of Violence Against Women (OVW) which directs VAWA funding, is beholden to the parameters of welfare reform. Because protection from abuse is omitted from the fatherhood/marriage promotion agenda, OVW and its cohorts advocate for "safety" in conjunction with father's access. What does that mean? The two goals are incongruous. How can women and children be "safe" when their abuser has unwelcomed contact and control? DV staff are well aware of the contradiction so they advance the idea that as long as dad does not physically assault mother and children during exchanges or in court venues, there is safety. Minimally, they advocate for "step visitation" or "neutral exchanges." Both methods leave children at risk while in the possession of incorrigible men.

Is it truly possible to limit the definition of safety? Is it possible to recover and stay safe when a perpetrator is a constant presence? DV staff have conceded women's and children's voices, concerns and experiences to their own economic self-interests. Alarmingly the condescension has resulted in DV staff working with the trade association and fatherhood to put protocols into place that will further draw subjects into the scheme.

In March of 2013, a roundtable discussion occurred amongst the top-most level of special interest groups: domestic violence, the trade association AFCC, NCJFCJ (judicial group) and child support.[38] Those in attendance included:

- Vicky Turetsky as Commissioner of the Office of Child Support Enforcement, Department of Health and Human Services.
- Peter Salem as Director of AFCC and author of court protocols.
- Lynn Rosenthal as the White House Advisor on Violence Against Women.
- Virginia Baran Lyons as head of The Custody Project under the Office of Violence Against Women.
- Nancy Ver Steegh as future President of AFCC and author of domestic violence court primers.
- Loretta Frederick as head of the Battered Women's Justice Project and recipient of OVW grants to influence court protocols.
- Maureen Sheeran as staff of NCJFCJ and developer of the Resource Center on Domestic Violence, Child Protection and Custody (1994).
- Jessica Pearson as Director of the Center for Policy Research and the author of numerous fatherhood playbooks funded by OCSE grants.
- Arthur Shienvold as a promoter of mediation and fellow of Pennsylvania's APA custody evaluation task force.

---

[38] "Roundtable on Domestic Violence Child Support Programs and Parenting Time Orders: Research, Practice, and Partnership Project" Meeting Synopsis, Prepared by Jessica Pearson, September 2013.

Numerous employees of family courts and domestic violence and trade association groups were also in attendance. Attachment B, pages 21-30, contains detailed biographies of the participants. One must look at the vast array of connections and influence of special interests in order to ferret out why women are subjected to further abuse by litigation and why children are placed in the hands of highly dangerous dads.

Attachment "D" OCSE's Fact Sheet on Family Violence Collaboration, pages 32-37 shows how fatherhood, domestic violence and child protection services work together to get even dads with a history of violence custody. The professed goal is to help mothers safely access child support, which the fact sheet acknowledges is a trigger for violence, while simultaneously increasing father's involvement [through custody awards]. Mothers unwittingly file for support only to trigger custody actions. Even uneducated fathers quickly learn that increasing custody decreases support obligation. The cycle of financial reward and punishment begins with the mere step of filing for support.

Attachment E, pages 28-31, contains critical thinking questions that ask "How can we address safety issues when establishing parenting time?" The answer is not to limit or control the abusers reach. OVW, OCSE, AFCC, and NCJFCJ never question "Should we protect children from further harm?" "How can we assure the safety, stability and nurturing of children?" "How can we adhere to due process requirements?"

The roundtable occurred for one reason: to forward the amount of custody orders written through the vehicle of child support offices. President Obama, as part of his 2014 budget proposal allocated $448 million over ten years, in addition to fatherhood AV grants, to require a custody order for every parent with a child support order. The budget permits IV-D reimbursement money to pay for the administrative costs of internal efforts – hearings, conferences, litigation services such as supervised visits and third-party appointment.

Fatherhood requirements resulted in increased custody awards to highly detrimental men. Domestic violence staff are well aware of the incongruity of goals. Even though many roundtable participants are members of the legal profession, there is no discussion of constitutional safeguards such as:

- ensuring due process,
- adherence to state custody laws that require abuse to be viewed as detrimental,
- the right to present valid evidence if alleging parental unfitness, and,
- the right to a quick, fair and just, hearing or trial.

Instead, domestic violence staff advocate for training opportunities and positions of consultation and collaboration. While it is well known by Ms. Frederick, Rosenthal, Baran Lyons, and Sheeran, that court employees and appointees are severely impaired in their understanding and consideration of the power dynamics behind these relationships, and that highly abusive males fight for custody -- at no point in the roundtable report does any staff speak-up and call-out the numerous tactics used by male supremacists and father's rights to win sole custody. DV legal experts do not explain that psycho-social abusers:

- Have a high probability of situational pedophilia when left unaccountable due to their psychological failings, over-inflated sense of self-importance, dehumanization of targets, and, lack of appropriate barriers.
- Are more likely to make false allegations against their victims, deny their actions, and portray themselves as the victim.

These character traits are omitted in participant's zeal to institute a mandatory custody mechanism within support offices. Ensuring adherence to ethical standards for judges, lawyers, and mental health appointees is not considered by roundtable participants, even though, Stienvold is a member of PA's psychological oversight organization. An NCJFCJ benchbook requiring safety to ethically be the first consideration in a best-interests standard - does not provide the groundwork for OCSE custody - even though Sheeran participated in the writing of this quantitative judge's guide.

The upper-most special interest group management that participated in this OCSE custody mandate roundtable left out talk of the cost of defending oneself in a highly contested custody case - a glaring omission - whilst running full speed ahead to conspire to influence court processes - hiding pre-determined outcomes within the support office.

AFCC Training on Abuse Classification

A third 2007 AFCC conference workshop reveals the beginnings of the collusion to classify abuse using Janet Johnston's model (page 4, conference brochure). An all-day (9-4) presentation was conducted in collaboration with National Council of Juvenile and Family Court Judges (NCJFCJ), Loretta Frederick of Battered Women's Justice Project (BWJP) and Janet Johnston, entitled *"Judicial Officers Institute: Domestic Violence and Differentiation."* This workshop followed The Wingspread Conference held by AFCC, NCJFCJ and attended by BWJP in February 2007. The workshop summary asks "What services are appropriate?" This appears to be another marketing event given the sole result of Wingspread was that *"All high conflict cases should have a co-parenting coordinator assigned to manage day-to-day decision-making and ongoing education."* Mothers have documented severe bias, mistreatment and ignoring of abuse under court ordered co-parenting arrangements.

Wingspread Conference: Abuse Classification

AFCC members have worked covertly to twist labeling of the existence and cause of abuse towards a model that favors fathers. Patriarchal males diminish the severity of abuse. Patriarchal males infiltrate existing groups in order to dictate the outcome of that organizations priorities and literature. In that manner, AFCC worked with NCJFCJ and BWJP to hold a conference on the subject of including domestic violence in custody litigation called *"The Wingspread Conference."*[39] Participants were asked to prepare for Wingspread by reading the article *"Differentiating Types of Domestic Violence: Implications for Child Custody"*[40] written by Nancy Ver Steegh, 2005. The article is based on Janet Johnston's typology of batterers.

The result of the conference is contained in *"Report From The Wingspread Conference on Domestic Violence and Family Courts"* written by Nancy Ver Steegh and Claire Dalton. The report is endorsed by AFCC, NCJFCJ, BWJP, and Janet Johnston. Page 12 of report states courts will have increased involvement with some families and a parenting coordinator should be appointed to make day-to-day decisions and continue to educate and resolve conflict. Again – abuse and protection is relegated to a dispute to be resolved by a third-party profiteer with questionable education and affiliations.

It is extremely important to read Lundy Bancroft's assessment of Johnston's/Ver Steegh's typology. In short, Bancroft makes three important points:

1) Anytime a women asserts herself or protects herself or

---

[39] "Report From the Wingspread Conference on Domestic Violence and Family Courts" Nancy Ver Steegh, Clare Dalton NCJFCJ – law professor involved in Navigating Domestic Violence packet – Family Court Review , July 2008 454-475. Vol. 46 no. 3

[40] "Differentiating Types of Domestic Violence: Implications for Child Custody" written by Nancy Ver Steegh, 2005.

the children – she is called the abuser – she is termed unsafe.
2) This typology does NOT assess HIS treatment of the children! A parent's ability to, and history of, care for the children is a paramount component of a judicial "best interests" custody determination.
3) Men who abuse their partner are more likely to abuse their children and have a higher risk of incest.

A description of the failure of this classification system is addressed in "*Motherless America: Confronting Welfare's Fatherhood Custody Program (pages 149-159)*."[41]

Child Support, Custody, and Abuse Classification

Further proof of tying classification of domestic violence to fatherhood initiatives comes from the AFCC published article "*Calculating Safety: Reckoning with Domestic Violence in the Context of Child Support Parenting Time Initiatives*" written by Ver Steegh and Davis. (Ver Steegh is a past President of AFCC and Davis of BWJP is currently on the editorial board of AFCC's newsletter.) [42]

Calculating Safety promotes the assessment of domestic violence of the parent only - not the children - at the onset of support litigation. When a party files for support – litigation begins; no support orders are issued without litigation whether or not a party has hired an attorney or is self-represented (pro se). *Calculating Safety* acknowledges that custody litigation is incorporated into support litigation. Ver Steegh and Davis attempt to resolve the problem of abusers automatically receiving custody by instituting a domestic violence assessment in the

---

[41] Motherless America: Confronting Welfare's Fatherhood Custody Program" Ludwig, Doreen, 2015, pages 149-159

[42] "Calculating Safety: Reckoning with Domestic Violence in the Context of Child Support Parenting Time Initiatives" written by Nancy Ver Steegh, & Gabrielle Davis, Family Court Review, Vol. 53 No. 2, Aril 2015 279-291.

support office.

Divorcing mothers file for, and initially receive, support payments (until custody is switched to father). The fatherhood program is portrayed as being for never-married parents. In truth, support does not differentiate – it would be unconstitutional.

In *Calculating Safety*, Davis and Ver Steegh acknowledge that abusers use custody litigation to further abuse (pg. 282) yet they do not inform the reader that if a party with children files for government assistance such as cash assistance, housing subsidies or food stamps, they are required to file for support payments. Therefore, filing for welfare assistance often begins custody litigation for poor women and children who may have never married the father.

Davis and Ver Steegh admit mediation has no due process and adherence to law (best interests) protection.

> *"Proceeding to court, instead of mediating, should be an easily available option for never-married parents. Traditional courts are not a panacea for parents with a history of domestic abuse, but for some they offer much needed protection in the form of due process guarantees, protective orders, enforcement mechanisms, and clear focus on the best interests of children."* (page 286)

Davis and Ver Steegh omit the fact that many jurisdictions operate quasi-judicial hearings where lawyers determine support and custody – often called "conciliation" hearings. These lawyers operate in lieu of third-party, off-site mediators.

Davis and Ver Steegh's proposed assessment tool relies on the Johnston/Johnson/Ver Steegh typology model discussed above. *Triage Intake Screen* is the vehicle marketed by AFCC -and implemented in AFCC member inundated courts.

NCJFCJ Benchbook[43]

Benchbook's are written to help judges make appropriate decisions on complex issues. Family court does not hold trials with twelve (12) jurors making custody determinations. One person, a judge, is permitted to singularly rule. Therefore, it is of the utmost important that the judge be informed and ethical. Benchbooks are written to aid in understanding the factors to consider in upholding this immense duty.

Unfortunately, family court judges have abdicated their legal responsibility to a plethora of third-party, profit-driven, special interests - many affiliates of trade association and father's rights networks. An "evaluator" is one such appointment - usually performed by a mental health practitioner. Because there are severe problems with custody evaluations - especially when abuse and unequal power define the relationship - the NCJFCJ (National Council of Juvenile and Family Court Judges) wrote a comprehensive, easy-to-follow, benchbook in 2004. The benchbook is so simple that it requires no additional grant money or payment to DV organizations for a day of hands-on training. A professional with a law degree can easily comprehend and implement this basic tool.

> ### *"How to Define DV*
>
> *Domestic Violence is a complex and confusing phenomenon. For purposes of this tool, as will become clear, we are defining it as a dynamic between parents whereby one partner seeks to control the other through the use of abusive patterns of behavior that operate at a variety of levels – emotional, psychological and physical.*

---

[43] "Navigating Custody and Visitation Evaluations in Cases with Domestic Violence: A Judges Guide" National Council of Juvenile and Family Court Judges, 2004.

The presence of this abusive dynamic will always be relevant to the question of what custody or visitation arrangement will serve the best interests of any children shared by the adult parties.

The untrained eye and ear do not reliably detect the abusive dynamics in relationships where violence is hidden or where most of the abuse is not physical in nature....The parties often hold radically different perceptions of their relationships and of one another; and abusers are often motivated to deny or minimize their abusive behavior. It is particularly important in these cases to test what the parties say against other available evidence.

The Legal Context

In cases involving known or suspected domestic violence, as in all contested custody cases, the court's fundamental task is to determine how each child has been affected by what has gone on inside the family, the quality of the child's relationship with each parent, each parent's capacity to meet the child's needs, and how best to assure the child's physical, psychological and emotional wellbeing going forward.

Judges are now almost universally under a statutory obligation to consider domestic violence as a factor when determining the best interests of children. It is why many judges are under a statutory obligation to presume that a perpetrator of domestic violence is not someone who should be given either joint or sole physical or legal custody of a child. For definitions of "domestic violence" underlying these specific statutory obligations may be narrower and more focused on physical violence than the broader definition we have proposed. But because domestic violence in the broader sense hurts children, it is incumbent on every judge in every custody or visitation decision based on the best interests of a child, regardless of particular statutory obligations to have an accurate picture of any violence or abuse in the parents' relationship, and to consider its implications for the child after the parents separate.

The Ethical Context: Safety First *[physical and emotional]*

"When you make a determination or approve a parental agreement about custody and visitation, you are trying to create a climate in which children can flourish, physically and emotionally. The safety of the parties and their children is a paramount consideration. Children do not flourish if they are not, or do not perceive themselves to be safe, or if they perceive their parents to be at risk. Parents who are fearful for their own safety may have a difficult time providing safety, security and effective parenting for their children."

In a section called "Resources: Links to Organizations" pages 26-27, the benchbook recommends AFCC as a group committed to dispute resolution, and lists OVW as working for welfare reform.

What's Wrong with Safety First?

I extracted from the benchbook to show that a custody determination is based on statutory obligation (the law) and ethics, and that domestic violence or abuse has a wider definition and impact. Joan Zorza, a lawyer who has represented numerous abused mothers and sexually molested children, identified egregious limits of the benchbook.[44] Zorza states the benchbook has a dearth of concern for sexual abuse of children, and, omits research that abusive men are 6.5 to 19 times more likely than other men to commit incest.[45]

---

[44] "Navigating Custody and Visitation Evaluations in Cases with Domestic Violence: A Judges Guide - A Mixed and Dangerous Tool" by Joan Zorza, Esq. 2005, 8 Sexual Assault Report, 49 (March/April 2005). Retrieved 12/16/17 @ http://www.thelizlibrary.org/liz/dangerous-tool.html

Zorza raises the danger for women and children from reliance on a family dynamic/systems approach even from the domestic violence community itself.

> "**Fails to DeBunk the Family Dynamic Approach** The discussion about "one partner seek[ing] to control the other through the use of abusive patterns or behaviors that operate at a variety of levels – emotional, psychological, and physical" (p. 8, cited above) **will lead the DV community to focusing on the coercive control aspects, while not noticing the more dangerous family dynamic approach on which most mental health professionals will focus.**"
>
> "Family dynamic proponents believe that any abuse problems are caused by the couple's dynamic, particularly their poor communication, and hence they are very likely to deny or trivialize the power, control and abuse issues, about which the guide seeks to educate".
>
> "Minimizing the DV or child abuse allegations, the family dynamic proponents are likely to blame mothers for exaggerating their abuse allegations, not emphasize the anger that victims feel (indeed, they treat it as a weakness and possibly an indication of instability and poor parenting), and assume that mothers raise abuse allegations to alienate their children from their other parent. Rather than protecting the victim, they are more likely to assume that therapy is needed to improve the couple's communication skills to solve the couple's problems. If the couple is sent to a therapist, the therapist is likely to share the same family systems dynamic perspective. **The result is the abuser will never have to confront his wrongdoing, impeding or preventing the**

---

[45] Bancroft, Lundy & Miller, Margaret. "The Batterer as Incest Perpetrator," 85, in The Batterer as Parent: Addressing the Impact of Domestic Violence on Family Dynamics, 2002

healing of the abuser, the victim and each of the other family members and further endangering the victim and children, as well as others exposed to the abuser in the future. " [emphasis added]

Zorza prophetically explains what occurs within family court ten years hence. Because of a grounding in family dynamics or systems - a lack of understanding of abuse and it's connection to entitlement - women and children are not permitted to heal. They are continually exposed to his bad behavior. All the while, family court affiliates continue to design and order "communication" and "mediation" then blame and punish those who have not been protected in the first place. Looking at the outcome of OVW grants to BWJP validates this ongoing failure of domestic violence community.

Family Dynamics/Systems: Founded on Patriarchy

The theory of Family Systems or Dynamics was developed by a psychiatrist, Murray Bowen, during the 1950's. Bowen surmised that family members were interdependent. One persons behavior and emotional response is predicated upon the behavior and emotional response of the other members of the family. The family should be viewed as a whole with a hierarchy. Members are not individuals but rather people reacting to the actions and emotions of other members. Therefore, counselors could teach members to change their behavior and reactions in order to effect change in their partner or child.

The flaw in family systems ideology comes from the era of its origin. In 1950 women were still beholden to husbands. Married women were not separate people but rather subjugated to him. Women were secondary, primarily housewives and child caregivers. Women were not individuals with their own intellect, wage earning capacity, opinions and ambition. Concluding that a women's insecurities drives dad's behavior – in order to detach from his wife's dependence he works longer hours – she pressures him to make more money so he drinks alcohol or hits her – may have seemed logical in 1959 – but the advancement of women's autonomy has clear implications to the family systems philosophy of viewing male/female relationships and behavior as reactionary and mutually dependent. Male abuse towards wives and children was not a factor in 1950. Women and children were still viewed as property. Subordinate. He was permitted to treat them any way he chose. He could have his wife institutionalized and lobotomized if she resisted his will. Yet, a psychiatrist built a world of ideology that makes her equally accountable for his actions – her behavior prompts his acts. Family systems is built around patriarchy – hierarchy - the male-dominant family.

Family systems ideology is heavily entrenched in family court. It is the foundation for how courts process perpetrators and subjects of family malfeasance. Rather than ask – "Why does he batter?" Family court affiliates ask – "What did she do to make him behave that way?" Instead of honoring a women's right to autonomy - mental health practitioners work to keep the family intact with father in a hierarchal position. A mother who refuses to stay in the unit is seen as a barrier. A mother who believes dad is unfit and wants to limit his contact is called a gatekeeper. Her concern is worrisome. His lack of appropriate parenting before separation is accepted because caregiving was previously her role. He is not blamed for his failure to appropriately nurture. After divorce he must be given every opportunity to be a father.

Everything is a system. In family court the family is dissolving – the family system exists no more and should not be forced to exist. Dissolution is an oft-taken option of women seeking liberation from his oppression. Today, many married adults were mature, separate adults before becoming parents. Some parents never marry. Some split-up before the birth. Yet - family court appointees still operate from a belief that the family is a unit that needs to be forced to be cohesive.

Abusers are first class manipulators. Abusers don't own their behavior. Entitlement is their inheritance.

An abusive marriage mimics a master/slave dynamic. It is oppression. The male is dominant - the female and children are expected to be submissive. The form that submission takes can be subtle and insidious. When an adult female retains enough self-worth she will leave. She will determine she will not be used nor will she let her children be destroyed. She wants to cut-off dependence as she pursues her dignity.

Should society still be making women the cause of male misbehavior? Are women still responsible for his character and conduct? Why is she scrutinized when his actions are a problem? Why is a male deemed fit for custody when it is a role he ignored until dissolution?

What about stability and nurturing?

The Centers for Disease Control views child maltreatment as a public health problem. In a booklet called *"Essentials for Childhood: Creating Safe, Stable, Nurturing Relationships and Environments"*[46] they list requirements for the healthy development of children's physical, emotional, social, behavioral and intellectual capabilities which effects their health as adults.

CDC considers:

> Safety: the extent to which a child is free from fear and secure from physical and psychological harm within their social and physical environment.
>
> Stability: the degree of predictability and consistency in a child's social, emotional and physical environment.
>
> Nurturing: the extent to which a parent or caregiver is available and able to sensitively and consistently respond to and meet the needs of their child.

These three factors are not part of custody determinations. It is

---

[46] https://www.cdc.gov/violenceprevention/childmaltreatment/essentials.html

common for children to suffer years of disruption and trauma, to have their attachment to their mother eliminated completely, to be sent to live with an abusive dad who has never provided care, has no interest in providing care and intends to concede mundane tasks to his parent, girlfriend, new wife, employee or child themself. Even shared parenting orders that require children to repeatedly switch residences and routines, provide anxiety and have the potential to cause irrevocable damage. Damage is amplified when a child is placed with an abusive dad merely for the benefit of lowering support obligation and fulfilling fatherhood program requirements.

Why is a mother diminished and dismissed when she has been providing the necessary stability and nurturing - even under difficult circumstances? Because she decided to strike out on her own? Because she recognized the harm the other parent is currently creating or will cause if she stays? Why is the non-nurturing dad exalted? Why is stability and continuity overlooked?

Addressing the best interests of a child by focusing on safety only continues to leave mothers and children in danger and fails to hold men accountable for their maltreatment.

Conclusion

Improvement cannot occur without proper definition of the problem. A government entity as important as family court should not operate with a profit-motive – hidden from view – unaccountable.

Let's build an alliance to ensure justice works for - not only the powerful and well-connected - but for those who need it most. Let's talk truth – not special interest dialect – because that's Trumpian Abuse!

***********(

If you enjoyed this book – share it. If you wish to support my work a donation via www.maccabuse.org is appreciated. It's a great way to communicate with me and build our organization.

ABOUT THE AUTHOR

Doreen Ludwig is the author of "Motherless America: Confronting Welfare's Fatherhood Custody Program" a self-styled memoir and research compendium. Doreen is the founder of the advocacy group Mothers Against Court Custody Abuse – MACCAbuse. www.MACCAbuse.org

Doreen is the proud daughter of three generations of Philadelphia fireman – men who showed by example that no fire is too big and no one is too important to be afraid of fighting.

www.ingramcontent.com/pod-product-compliance
Lightning Source LLC
Chambersburg PA
CBHW052302220526
45471CB00001B/450